The Saga of
The *Steam Ship*
Great Britain

The Saga of

The
Steam Ship

Great Britain

John O'Callaghan

Rupert Hart-Davis   London

Granada Publishing Limited
First published 1971 by Rupert Hart-Davis Ltd
3 Upper James Street London WIR 4BP

ISBN 0 246 64089 8
Printed in Great Britain by Northumberland Press Ltd
Gateshead

Contents

For *CHRISTINE,*
CITY CLIPPER

Illustrations

Panoramic view of the *Great Britain* in the Great Western Dock.

The *Great Britain* back in the dock where she was built.

The *Great Britain*'s winches.

Plywood patches over the great crack on the starboard side.

Skeleton of the interior.

Cleaning her hull in the dock.

Foreword

When it was announced that Mr Jack Hayward would pay to bring home the SS *Great Britain* some newspapermen reacted as if it was their money he was wasting. This curious animus did not ruffle the members of the Great Britain Project who obviously felt that nobody's money could be put to better use. But unless you had access to a handful of experts it was hard to discover why an ancient and little-known hulk in the Falkland Islands should matter so much. This book is an answer to that question.

In national terms it is the story of how Britain altered course from wood and sail to iron and steam in shipbuilding and annihilated American supremacy in merchant shipping. Between 1840 and 1892 Britain's mercantile tonnage rose 210 per cent and British ships then carried 56 per cent of the world's goods. The only token that remains of America's dominance in wooden clippers is her knack of making unbeatable ocean racing yachts.

In recounting the long and dramatic career of the *Great Britain* I have had the generous help of Mr George Maby at the Wills Memorial Library, Bristol; the Great Britain Project, in particular Lord Strathcona whose diary of the recovery forms a central part of the last chapter; and Lt-Cdr James Richard, RN, for valuable technical advice. Mr John Corin smoothed a path to early Port of Bristol minute books. Thanks are due also to the British Maritime Museum particularly for making available many pictures.

From a most exuberant Australian mail-bag Mr T. G. Atkinson, of Elizabeth Bay, NSW, Miss A. D. Mathews, of Glen Iris, Victoria, and Miss Gladys Robinson, of Brisbane, must stand proxy for thanks to all who so trustingly sent diaries, tickets, and other mementoes. Captain R. E. Holden, of Barbados, alerted me to the Liverpool Compass Committee. The Mitchell Library in Sydney, and the State Library of Victoria in Melbourne sent well-chosen photo-copies from their archives which acknowledge the importance of the *Great Britain* as something of a founding instrument of modern Australia.

In preparation for an expected recovery to San Francisco, that city's maritime museum had prepared an extensive dossier on the *Great Britain*. After generously withdrawing their fairly advanced preparations for taking the vessel to San Francisco in face of the British project's stronger claim, the museum has followed this up by sending to the project all the material it had collected. Access to it has helped me greatly in writing this book.

Original spellings have been retained in quotations from contemporary journals, not to demean the writers but to keep as much as possible of the original flavour; for consistency Cobh is called by its former British name of Queenstown.

The Saga of
The *Steam Ship*
Great Britain

CHAPTER I

Launched and Trapped

Prince Albert caught a six o'clock train from Paddington to Bristol on the morning of 19 July 1843 to launch the steamship *Great Britain*. His Prince Consort status was appropriate to christening the world's largest and most revolutionary ship. As a man with a technical bent he could appreciate the purpose and ingenuity of innovations like fold-down masts, the vessel's double bottom, and watertight bulkheads. The all-iron fabric and screw propeller were the major and most advertised novelties in a ship of 2,984 tons displacement—up to then they had been used together only experimentally in large vessels and to a limited commercial extent in ships seven times smaller than the *Great Britain*. In addition the new ship had a balanced rudder—the very beginnings of power-assisted steering at sea—and an electric speed and distance log; both these refinements were ahead of their time.

The 19 July 1843 was the day marine engineering made the great leap forward into modern times. Lower down the scale it was the day when Bristol fell from the front rank of British ports. The city had the railway from London, now it had the most advanced ship yet built to carry passengers to America by the shortest and most convenient route. Yet the vision of the Bristol Dock Company had become so clouded that the significance of becoming the transatlantic ferry terminal passed unnoticed. Liverpool took the trade and the *Great Britain* for good measure.

The Prince faced a long day of protocol in a distant and grimy part of the kingdom. If there was a worry, it was not about Bristol's commercial future, but over the city's ill-fame as a centre for violent riots. The last and worst of these took place 12 years before as part of the Reform Bill unrest. Getting to Bristol was an adventure, too, in 1843—118 miles to be covered at the prodigious rate of 45 m.p.h. Only 15 years before many had agreed that 30 m.p.h. would prove fatal to the human frame. To quell any incipient unease the Great Western Railway put its two greatest assets on the locomotive footplate—Mr Daniel Gooch, the locomotive chief, and Mr I. K. Brunel, the line's engineer, and designer of the *Great Britain*.

The journey took two hours and 40 minutes. This did not include a breathless stop at Bath to exchange civilities with that city's chief citizens on the station platform; it added six minutes to journey time. The humble as well as the mighty took advantage of the new benefits of rapid travel. Notorious London pickpockets were seen at work on Bristol station. Some were arrested by London police also making use of the new mobility. 'If I'd known you were to be here,' said one thief when he was arrested, 'I would have stayed in Town and had a field day.' In other respects Bristol was as bright as it could be made, lavishly decorated with garlands and triumphal arches. The *Bristol Mirror*'s versifier wrote:

> *In Temple Street wonders were everywhere seen,*
> *The fronts of the houses were really washed clean.*

After breakfasting in the GWR directors' room at the station, the launching party set out on a long procession towards the dock. William Prideaux of Merriott Vicarage described the scene in a letter: 'The Prince took off his hat repeatedly. I think he must have tired his arm. He is a very handsome young man, though he looked rather pale and tired. I should wonder how it could be otherwise as he had been travelling ever since six o'clock; there was very little cheering I thought, though in the newspapers of course it said that he was received with the loud and continued acclamations of the multitude.' Bristol's lack of voice may have been due to uncertainty, as the *Bristol Mirror*'s poet hinted:

> *To find folks who had waited for hours or more,*
> *Without ever stirring from window or door,*
> *And their love and their loyalty longed to evince,*
> *Not making their minds up quite 'Which is the Prince?'*
> *Some thought it was this one, some it was that,*
> *And many the man in the monstrous cocked hat.*

If there was any doubt about the identity of Prince Albert

there can have been none about his goal when he arrived at the Great Western Steam Ship Company's yard after a tour made memorable for the Prince by seeing two men in a basket-car traversing the slender bar then linking the ends of the unfinished Clifton suspension bridge. There was the *Great Britain* towering out of the water, riding high because very little of her machinery had been put aboard. Her funnel was a dummy and Brunel proposed that a propeller, quite unlike those then the subject of patent claims, should be added for authenticity—made of wood. But impressions that she was excessively high out the water owe something to contemporary unfamiliarity with anything but designs in wood.

That the *Great Britain* was a strange sight even to eyes familiar with ships is clear from this report of a pre-launch glimpse in the *Nautical Magazine*: 'What can I say of this gigantic vessel. I have had but a transient view of her but sufficient to impress me with the belief that she will prove to be something out of the common build of sea-going craft. There is no other steamer, nay vessel of any class I believe I may safely say, with such an extraordinary over-hanging bow. And as to the cut-water, it does not measure more than an inch, I should think, judging from eye-sight. In thickness, indeed it may be called a razor cut and if thinness be an advantage in dividing the fluid she has it in perfection. Her whole monstrous body will be light compared with a wood built vessel of the same tonnage as the plates seem to me not much to exceed the above measure [one inch] if indeed they are so thick. No doubt they are each and all of good stuff and will bear a punch indenting rather than cracking by collision with other materials. The wing flaps of the screw are curious looking things difficult indeed to be described by any but a mechanic.'

The Prince had the builder's yard superintendent, Mr Thomas Guppy who was also a director, to explain the wonders of the *Great Britain* to him, and Mr Guppy said he had been quizzed 'with many and minute inquiries respecting her construction and capabilities'. A banquet lunch for 600 followed set out in the dock workshop and rather spoiled by tramping soldiers who made the speeches inaudible.

Lunch—and a particularly nasty shower—over, the Prince came forward to perform the ceremony for which the word 'un-docking' was used in place of launch. Mainly because of her colossal weight—over 1,000 tons of metal went into her hull alone—the *Great Britain* was not to be launched in the usual slipway style. She had been built in a dock especially dug out— a graving dock—so that she could be floated without being conventionally launched. But to simulate the effect of a launch the ship was to be towed out of her dock into the general harbour by a tug, the *Avon*, also propelled by a screw. The Prince was to smash a bottle of champagne on the *Great Britain*'s starboard bow—the ship would float out and citizens occupying 10,000 five-shilling seats on the opposite side of the vessel, having seen nothing of this, would then catch their first glimpse of the Consort. 'The sudden and mutual recognition of each other by Prince and people,' said the *Bristol Mercury*, 'will not form one of the least pleasing incidents in the proceedings of the day.'

A hitch ruined this plan. First, Prince Albert stood down and allowed Mrs Miles, mother of a Bristol MP, to swing the bottle; six years before to the day she had launched the *Great Western*, the pioneer paddle steamer the *Great Britain* was to join on the transatlantic run. Mrs Miles threw the bottle, missed the target, and the wine fell intact into the water. The blame—though some said it was plain clumsiness—was put on the tug *Avon*. She had started pulling too soon against the *Great Britain*'s mooring ropes, the tow rope broke and slewed the ship at the critical moment. The Prince effectively smashed a reserve bottle, tipping the contents on dockers below fending off the ship. But the broken tow rope prevented the 'mutual recognition' taking place, for the Prince left to catch his train back to London. It left at 4.17 and arrived in London at 6.57 when the Prince 'expressed himself warmly in approval' of having travelled 236 miles in 12 hours and spent six hours in Bristol. The disappointed five-shilling ticket holders along with the guinea lunch eaters defrayed the whole cost of the event.

More distant spectators had other problems, as William Prideaux described: 'We had several storms and it was such a curious sight to see several thousand umbrellas twisted all together, the hill in fact looked like a large ants' nest; however it was not a very good place so by Mr Cross's influence we got admission to a range of seats just outside the Clifton National School room where there was a nice view of the vessel. But we had to wait a long time, more than an hour I think, during which time down came a very heavy storm which thinned the seats; so taking an opportunity I slipped down front. Next to me sat a fat old lady or rather respectable person who as she happened to have no umbrella very kindly offered to hold mine, which I was silly enough to let her do, by which means I got wet through on one side, I wished I had not been so kind. It cleared up just as the vessel was being towed out by a little steamer, the *Avon*, worked like herself by the Archimedian screw, as her own works are not used; the papers say she was christened by the Prince hurling a bottle of champagne at her, but in reality Mrs Miles tried to perform the operation, and being clumsy or nervous instead of throwing the bottle let it drop out of her hands into the water; so the vessel was not christened at all, perhaps it is a bad omen; she is now to be seen at a shilling a head.'

'A bad omen?' The Great Western Steam Ship Company could be excused for thinking that something had blighted the birth of their sleek, dark-hulled ship with only false black and white gun ports on her sides, and false galleries on her stern making a gesture to the age she had left behind. Still firmly fixed in the Nelson era, the Bristol Dock Company were not to be distracted by decorative concessions from the fact that the *Great Britain* was too wide at 50 ft. 6 in. to get out of their harbour. The manoeuvring and hairsplitting that this provoked kept the ship uselessly imprisoned for eight months and cost her owners a season's trade.

After a little bother because a baulk of timber jammed in her keel, the *Great Britain* went from the graving dock into the floating harbour. To get to the river Avon she had to pass through a single lock into the Cumberland Basin, and then through one of a pair of locks into the river. Most of the argument revolved about getting her through the first single lock, 45 ft. wide in theory but actually narrower. But she was too wide for the outer lock as well.

The answer to the inevitable question 'did they build her without measuring the lock?' is no. Agitation for bigger locks had begun before she was conceived; Brunel did surveys for wider locks at the dock directors' request. With the growth of paddle steamers wider locks had to come. But Isambard Brunel junior indicates in his biographical notes on his father that the actual lock width was always in mind. 'When it was first deter-

mined to build the *Great Britain* of iron it was intended that
she should be of the usual full form below the waterline. However it was ascertained that with such a midships section she
could not pass through the upper lock in the basin, and it was
therefore resolved by the directors of the GWSSCo (minute, 25
July 1839) to apply after consultation with Mr Brunel to the
Dock Company to make a temporary alteration to the top wall.
This proposal was, however, abandoned and her midship section
was expressly designed to allow her, when light, free passage
through the upper lock.

'But for the convenience of the company, and the trade of the
port, as well as from considerations of economy it was (in 1841)
deemed advisable to put the engines on board before the ship left
the Float. Eventually the directors, after considering the great
inconvenience which would result from putting in the engines
in the Cumberland Basin, which was only about twice as long
as the ship herself, determined to put them in place before
passing the ship through the lock. From the necessity there was
of occasionally letting off the water it is obvious that a ship of
about half the length of the basin would have been for the time
she continued there immensely in the way of the business of the
port.

'The determination to fit the engines within the Float rendered it necessary that a certain degree of accommodation should
be afforded in widening the top of the lock as the ship was brought
down by the weight of the engines so that her wide part no
longer cleared the top wall as it was designed to do. But Mr
Brunel, being consulting engineer to the docks, no difficulty
was apprehended, nor it is almost certain would there have been
any but that at the time permission had to be asked there was a
conflict at the dock board between the proprietory directors and
the city-interest directors which led eventually (1848) to the
docks being bought by the city.'

Now a word about the villains of the piece. Bristol Dock
Company was brought into being by a series of Acts of Parliament after 1803 to deal with a £580,000 development scheme to
divert the Avon, and create a permanent pool in her old bed
where ships could float all the time instead of lying on the mud
between tides. The management of the harbour was vested in
representatives of three bodies together forming the board—the
town council, the Society of Merchant Venturers, a 300-year-old

trade protection society, and representatives of subscribers to the dock capital.

They did not make a very cohesive unit. Having prostrated themselves with the big improvement scheme finished only in 1809, and which failed to restore Bristol's trade, they were not eager to hear of new ways to accommodate the trade which had used them so perversely. Their attitude is well described in Charles Wells' *History of the Port of Bristol* dealing with problems that arose over the *Great Western*, the GWSSCo's only previous ship, launched in 1837: 'The new ship could not safely use the harbour and had to lie in Kingroad (part of the Severn at the mouth of the Avon) to discharge and load by means of smaller craft. The Dock Company exacted their dues of £106 per trip, and as much more on the cargo, holding that they were not competent to make abatements. Besides, having carried out their obligations under the Acts for improving the harbour, it would be manifestly unjust, they said, to be defeated of their profits by the building of ships too large to enter that harbour.'

Less sympathy was forthcoming for the ship that was too large to get out. That there had been a lot of acrimony over the *Great Western*'s dues did not help. But £2,500 *had* been paid by the GWSSCo in dues and it felt—in view of the small return it got for it—that this ought to have sweetened the atmosphere. Unfortunately the *Great Britain* began life by incurring a troublesome debt. To breach the walls of her building dock safely, the water in the Float had to be lowered. A six-foot drop was arranged to fit in with Dock Company workings. Circumstances at the *Great Britain* dock required a deeper drop in the level than this and damage was done to the ship *Augusta*, bringing a bill of £312. 17s. 10d. which the GWSSCo resisted paying. There was thus a less than perfect relationship between the GWSSCo and the Dock Company, and an inhibiting tension in the Dock Company itself between the public service elements and the profit minders.

For five months after she was 'undocked' the *Great Britain* continued fitting out alongside the Gas Works Steps on the north side of the float from where she had been built. It was not until the beginning of 1844 that approaches were made to the Dock Company, and on New Year's day a three-man delegation from the GWSSCo put the problem before the dock directors asking 'that the gates and bridges at the Upper Lock of the Cumberland

Basin be removed for the space of a fortnight and that the bridges at the lower large lock be also removed as long as may be necessary to allow the *Great Britain* to pass into the river, and further that for the purpose of enabling her to pass through the locks two or three courses of masonry should be removed and replaced—the Steamship Company to defray every expense.'

This unvarnished request was more than the dock directors could assimilate at a routine meeting. They called for a written document—'this application is of far too much importance to receive the determination of the board merely on a verbal representation'. A special meeting was called for 12 February at which the proposal was put and passed. Or rather a motion denying permission was put and lost by 13 votes to five. Approval was conditional upon the GWSSCo getting the gates back, the walls repaired, and everything in working order by 19 March.

On 19 February however the minority opposition to this co-operative spirit had worked itself up into a mood of no surrender behind two of the directors for what were called the proprietors —those with investments in the docks. These two, Mr Joseph Cookson, oddly, a subscribing owner of the *Great Western*, and Mr James George, delivered a protest against the previous meeting's approving motion. The formal protest said that the dock company had no authority to sanction the alterations under its enabling Acts. There would, said Cookson and George, be inconvenience to shipping, water would flow up on the quays and into people's cellars, and the proposal was illegal, and contrary to public policy and convenience.

The protesters put forward another reason for not allowing the lock gates and walls to be tampered with. The *Great Britain* could, they said, 'be lifted out of the water sufficiently high to pass through without removing the gates'. This was the first open reference to the pontoon technique of raising the *Great Britain* and it was just 126 years ahead of its time. Perhaps because it was such a futuristic idea, the pontoon proposal later became significant to the release of the vessel.

In their dealings with the Bristol Dock Company, the Steamship Company directors' demeanour was appropriate to humouring a prickly dotard. The inflated alarms of Messrs Cookson and George were ludicrous. According to Steamship Company estimates removing and replacing the dock wall masonry would cost £190, with perhaps £40 for new stone to put in place of any broken or lost. But the GWSSCo offered to put £1,000 in the hands of the Dock Company secretary as a security for the work being done properly.

This was not enough. The Dock directors wanted an open-ended indemnity 'against all consequences that may result either to the Dock Company, or any other party ... being sufficient, legally, to bind the funds and property of the GWSSCo'. And although the dock directors had previously allowed £200 worth of alterations to bridges to let the *Great Western* in and out of the floating harbour without any indemnity, they now wanted to opt out of any responsibility for letting the *Great Britain* out.

They had taken legal advice and been told the alterations to the docks would be illegal under the terms of the Dock Company Acts, but that it would be possible, illegal though they were, to be indemnified against their consequences. Full cover could be obtained, however, from the GWSSCo only by getting 'a sufficient number of the partners in the GWSSCo, of undoubted responsibility, to enter into a joint and several bond to indemnify the Dock Company'. There was the germ of a practical reason for the Dock Company's attitude. Unluckily for the Steamship Company the outer lock gates, leading from the Basin to the Avon, had become jammed by an obstruction early in 1844; to move it the Basin had to be drained. 'Had the proposed alterations of the works been then in operation not only would the entrance basin but the whole floating harbour would have been dry,' wrote the Dock directors.

Disinclined to risk personal ruin by the total commitment required of them, the directors of the GWSSCo made a last offer to the Dock Company on the 4 March 1844 through Mr Guppy. In a letter which took most of the sting even out of the practical objections to the lock widening he said 'I am authorised by the GWSSCo to propose to contribute £1,000 towards the permanent widening of the upper part of the locks'. Even this generous offer brought no response from the Dock Company which had declared on 19 February that 'this board has nothing to propose'.

On 25 March the GWSSCo announced that it had been advised 'to solicit the mediation of the Board of Trade in the removal of difficulties which impede the transit of the *Great Britain* through the Dock Company's works'. This was done in 'no hostile spirit' but to avoid application to Parliament.

In their application the GWSSCo directors said that times had

changed and that now not a single steamer from ports as far
apart as Hamburg and Cadiz could get into Bristol because the
lock gates were too narrow. Blessed with 'railroads' and shipbuilding facilities (not least the GWSSCo's own yard) Bristol's
lack of access prevented orders being placed. They pleaded
national defence—naval vessels damaged by storm or enemy
action could not come into Bristol for repair. Liverpool's locks
were now 70 ft. wide, and Bristol should be urged by Her
Majesty's Government to make improvements 'sufficient to
admit ordinary paddle wheel steamers of the present day most
of which are far wider than the *Great Britain*'. The *Bristol
Mercury* reported on 30 March 1844 that the Board of Trade
said it would mediate in the dispute and had appointed the
eminent engineer Mr Cubitt as arbiter. On 9 April the Board
wrote to say that 'my Lords do not perceive that the demands of
the Dock Company are unreasonable and they trust it may be
found practicable to comply with them'.

In the pause that followed newspapers took up the cry for the
Great Britain's release. The *Bristol Mercury* wrote. 'Each
succeeding day's delay adds to the ridiculousness of the poor
Great Britain's position. London laughs, Liverpool grins, and a
universal titter is spreading through the whole commercial
world. This is not pleasant. Bristol had not gained anything in
a pecuniary point of view by building the *Great Western* and
Great Britain, but she at least earned a high and honourable
distinction as being the first to solve the problem of the steam
navigation of the Atlantic ... and having built the largest steam
ship which has yet come from the hands of man. The imprison-
ment of the *Great Britain* is but a "lame and impotent conclusion" to such great doings.'

In the *Railway Magazine* the Dock Company was attacked as
'this do-nothing body'—not a vessel from Liverpool or Glasgow
could get into Bristol. And the last verse of a poem by
'Sympathizer' read:

> Oh dock directors hear my sad appeal
> Break down your walls and open wide your doors
> And let me once the joys of freedom feel,
> And never will I trouble Bristol more.

For the ship's owners the delay was acutely embarrassing

because it cost money they could not afford. One of the reasons why the *Great Britain* had been four years on the stocks was because funds had run short. Now Cunard in Liverpool had four transatlantic steamers in operation each cutting into the *Great Western*'s profits. At the March 1844 AGM the piecemeal sale of the yard that had built the *Great Britain* was imminent.

Thoughts turned again to ways of getting the ship through the locks and on the 10 May Brunel wrote: 'I saw Mr Guppy yesterday and he will send me tracings of the proposed floating apparatus. I can state generally however at present that I approve entirely of the plan of forcing one large floating vessel under the bottom of the *Great Britain* and although it may be more expensive than the plan I had proposed of air vessels it will unquestionably be a more certain and a more easily managed and a more safe mode of proceeding.'

Hearing of the deadlock at Bristol a Mr E. Huston wrote to the Board of Trade saying that he was 'willing to enter into arrangements with the directors of the GWSSCo for lifting the *Great Britain* by his patented Flexible Air Tight Cases whereby all damage to the Bristol Dock Company works will be avoided'. In the *Bristol Mercury* of 24 April it was announced that the Steam Ship Company had resumed the idea of getting the ship out with tanks built in her building dock to form a cradle round her; 'the whole will assume the appearance of a flat bottomed boat'. Other offers of help were received.

As the summer of 1844 approached reference to virtuoso buoyancy devices dwindled. The Dock Company instead got together with Brunel—whether driven by Brunel, public opinion, or common sense is not minuted—to go seriously into the question of widening the locks. Brunel had surveyed these locks in 1840 after the town council had passed a resolution 'that it is essential to the trade of the port that the entrance to the floating harbour should be made wider'.

On 3 June 1844 Brunel wrote to Capt Claxton 'as regards the advice I am going to give them [the Dock Co] as to the rebuilding of the small lock'. He wanted from Claxton details of the dimensions of ships using the port, and the pressures acting on the gates. The letter ends: 'I think of recommending a thoroughly good lock—of course remember this has *no reference* whatever to *Great Britain*.' By the early Autumn plans had been endorsed and tenders invited.

So a different atmosphere and set of circumstances existed when Mr John William Miles, member of a senior Bristol family, and GWSSCo director, arrived at a meeting of the Dock Company on 9 September 1844 on behalf of the directors of the GWSSCo.

Miles 'applied for permission to make such alterations in the lock between the Float and the Cumberland Basin as might be found requisite for the passage of the *Great Britain* through the same in the course of the next month with a view to relieving the company from the necessity of adopting the dangerous alternative of taking the vessel through by means of lifting apparatus'. The proposal was asked for in writing with details of the indemnity proposed. On 13 September the directors of the GWSSCo resolved that if they got 'every facility whether by means of their Act of Parliament or otherwise' for getting out the *Great Britain* they were prepared fully to indemnify the Dock Company against all consequences.

This was considered by a special meeting on 16 September 1844 when the Dock Company board decided that 'the risk of damage to the company's works and injury to citizens and mercantile interests in general by any accident that might happen to the *Great Britain* in the course of her being passed through the locks in question by lifting power would be greater than would be likely to arise from the course proposed by the GWSSCo in their application'. This application was for a passage through both the inner lock and the one into the Avon; the inner lock had to be back in full working order by 9 November, and the other lock by 14 December with a penalty of £100 for each day's delay after that.

Several forces were at work on the dock directors. On 22 July another motion demanding that the outer lock be widened had come down from a town council meeting. It evoked this astonishing response: 'Assuming it to be understood that such resolution amounts to an approval and sanction of the recommendations as to the widening of the outer lock contained in Mr Brunel's report of 15 June, and that it does not recognise or imply any liability on the part of this company to enlarge the locks according as the accommodation of the trade of the port may require, such a resolution (as the town council sent down) may be received and entered on the minutes.'

Apprehensive about the damage the *Great Britain* was likely to cause floating out on her own bottom, the dock directors were clearly more afraid of what might happen in an effort to get her out on water-borne stilts, whether Brunel's pontoon, or Huston's Flexible Air Tight Cases. But most of all the Dock Company was moved to ease the *Great Britain* out by the capitulation of the GWSSCo directors to the demand for total indemnity. Bonds of Indemnity were signed on 14 October 'such bonds being for £100,000'. An enormous sum for a job originally estimated at less than £200—and big for an operation that actually cost £1,330. 4s. 9d.

After six months during which she earned only showpiece revenue at a shilling a head, the *Great Britain* came within sniffing distance of the sea on Saturday, 26 October when she passed through the lock from the Float to the Cumberland Basin. Work restoring the lock walls and gates—she was too long for the lock as well as too wide—started the same day. While waiting for the especially high tides in December the engines were tested; the high tides would, it was hoped, take her through the outer locks with minimum interference with masonry, and none with the gates. Then all superfluous stores and gear, including topmasts and yards, were put ashore.

Before daylight on Wednesday, 11 December a large crowd waited in the rain to see the end of the world's lengthiest launch. There was an easterly wind blowing which reduced the water level. No allowance had been made for this falling off in the height of the water, wrote a reporter. 'When the vessel was about half way through there was a hitch. The impediment in this instance was quickly removed and again she moved forward, but only a few yards when her progress again was impeded.

'It was no time for deliberation; the tide was at its height and had it receded in the most trifling degree, the vessel would have been doomed. It was therefore wisely, because promptly, resolved to 'try back', and the precaution having been taken to have a steam tug at either end of her, she was soon removed from her perilous situation, after which the multitude quietly dispersed.' The reporter blamed the east wind for the mishap, others blamed the engine-room staff on the *Great Britain* being unable to resist filling her boilers with clear fresh water, thus bringing her down in the water.

There was a fractionally higher tide that Wednesday evening. Brunel, who took charge of operations, did not rely on it. He recruited a huge gang of workers tearing out walls, coping stones, and the road bridge over the lock. In the evening the crudely enlarged lock was illuminated by lighted tar barrels when the tug *Samson* pulled the *Great Britain* through without any hindrance. Brunel then wrote to railway speculators in Wales:

'I am detained here by event which will I hope prove sufficient to excuse to the directors of the South Wales for my non-attendance. We have had an unexpected difficulty with the *Great Britain* this morning. She stuck in the lock; we did get her back. I have been hard at work all day altering the masonry of the lock. Tonight our last tide and we have succeeded in getting her through but being dark we have been obliged to ground her outside and I confess I cannot leave her until I see her afloat and all clear of our difficulties. I have, as you will admit, much at stake here, and I am too anxious to leave her.'

Next day the *Great Britain* was towed down to the Severn estuary, her engines started, and Brunel's anxieties laid at rest by a speed of 11 knots at 16½ r.p.m. from the engine against a strong headwind. That evening 70 visitors 'sat down in the spacious saloon to a most excellent dinner'. It took the Dock Company four years to finish the widening work begun by Brunel's gang on the lock.

Surviving records of the performance of the *Great Britain*'s first engines suggest that they did not achieve their rated 1,000 horsepower. Their shortcomings were not so much culpable as a natural consequence of being early in the field. Thermodynamics barely existed in the 1840s. Brunel and Guppy tried to save fuel by admitting steam to the cylinders at its full 5 lb. per sq. in. for only a quarter or even a sixth (instead of two-thirds to three-quarters) of the piston stroke. Lots of experiments for making small amounts of steam do a maximum of work had been tried on the *Great Western*'s engines.

It was not appreciated that greatly expanded steam underwent a proportionate drop in temperature. Some of the power in the following intake of steam was lost through condensation on the piston and cylinder walls; because of the low pressures cylinders had to be of large cubic capacity which aggravated the problem. More power was lost because the widely-used slide valve meant new steam came into the cylinder through the same opening as the exhausted steam—40°F cooler—had just left. By this time many land engines had steam jackets around the cylinder to help with the condensation problem. Space and weight considerations inhibited this at sea. Every inch saved on the piston stroke saved 3 in. in overall engine length which meant short-stroke, big-bore cylinders with inevitable losses through unjacketable cylinder ends and pistons.

Giving the engine a short power phase meant that the bulk and strength needed to absorb the stresses applied for a quarter of the time had to be carried superfluously for three quarters of the time. So there were irreconcilable elements in the marine engineer's pursuit of perfection; he used a little steam expansively to save fuel, but without high pressure or remedies for heat loss his intentions were thwarted. High pressure in ocean-going ships had to await the end of salt water for raising steam —an improvement that came with efficient condensers around 1865. Salt water had the added snag of leaving heavy brine deposits in the boilers which prevented the water from absorbing furnace heat quickly and led to boiler plates being weakened by overheating with consequent real dangers of explosion.

Discounting the £53,000 invested in her building yard and engine factory, the *Great Britain* as she stood ready to begin her career had cost £117,295—£73,000 for the hull and engines, £18,000 for rigging, fittings and stores, and £26,000 going to interest charges, rates, and other incidentals. It was a large investment; but with her five watertight compartments, electric log indicator in the saloon, her double bottom, seven lifeboats capable of carrying 400, and 26 water closets—these advanced provisions on top of her basic uniqueness—the *Great Britain* represented value for money.

In the league table of marine engine fuel efficiency the *Great Britain* shows that she was very much of the 1840 generation. Allowing—in view of doubts expressed about how much power the first engine could produce—that the indicated horsepower as well as the nominal was 1,000, if Guppy's estimate of 40 tons of coal used in 24 hours is right then the *Great Britain* used 3.7 lb. of coal per indicated horsepower per hour—not at all bad. Guppy admitted, however, that this was a guess based on the first returns during the maiden voyage. If the worst later figure— 80 tons per 24 hours—is used the figure becomes a very poor 7.4 lb. If 60 tons is a fair compromise the coal used per horsepower per hour was 5.6 lb. These are some figures from other typical ships: PS *Liverpool* (1835) 5.21 lb.; PS *Scotia* (1861) 3.6 lb.; RMS *Mauretania* (1906) 1.6 lb. on coal, 1.05 lb. on oil in 1929; *Empress of Canada* (1931) 0.7 lb.; *QE 2* (1967) 0.56 lb.

CHAPTER II

Revolution on the Stocks

On 28 May 1838, only five weeks after the *Great Western* set out from the River Avon for New York on her maiden voyage the GWSSCo decided to lay down the keel for its second ship. She was to be called the *City of New York* and an order was placed for a large amount of African timber. As a concession to Brunel's wishes, and to a greater profitability, the only stipulation that accompanied the decision in principle to build a sister paddle steamer for the *Great Western* was that she would have twice the carrying capacity—2,000 tons. The news was not made public until 28 September 1838 when the press wrongly said that the new vessel was to be the same size as her predecessor. Like the *Great Western*, the new ship was to be constructed by a Building Committee consisting of Brunel, Guppy, and Captain Christopher Claxton RN, managing director of the GWSSCo, helped by William Paterson, Bristol shipbuilder.

Before any serious dispositions had been made about building the ship, and only a month after the intention to build had become known in September, the question of making her of iron was raised by Thomas Guppy with the GWSSCo Board. He and Brunel had made some calculations and in a joint report tried to estimate the cost and efficiency of iron as a shipbuilding material. With the *Great Western* scooping the Atlantic passenger pool—in September 1838 she made a trip with 143 passengers, better than she would ever do again—the GWSSCo directors felt that they could afford to delay and indulge the genius of their engineer. They asked Captain Claxton and Paterson to make a few exploratory voyages in iron ships. With the benefit of only five years hindsight Claxton wrote of those experiments:

'The superiority of iron over wood-built vessels is so far admitted as to render it almost unnecessary at the present day to mention the reasons which induced the directors to give it preference; but five years ago when they boldly decided to build their ship of iron the case was different. The directors then instituted the most searching inquiries without experience, and with scarcely a theory to guide them. The writer of these pages, then Managing Director, made several passages in the *Rainbow* and in other iron vessels accompanied by Mr Paterson who afterwards furnished the lines for the *Great Britain*, for the purpose of testing their sea-going qualities, trying errors and variations of compasses, making investigations respecting oxidation, fouling of bottoms, buoyancy, and stability under canvas. It became manifest that iron would afford greater strength, greater buoyancy, and more capacity at less expense than wood. In capacity alone, for instance, the *Great Britain* gains considerably more than 600 tons.

'To make this clear to everyone it is necessary to suppose the angle-irons or ribs, the shelves, etc., etc., rolled out and added to the thickness of the plates forming her sides—when an average thickness of two feet of timber is represented by an average thickness of $2\frac{1}{2}$ inches of iron with far better ties, more compact framework, and far greater strength altogether than wood can, under any circumstances, afford. It was shewn likewise that dry-rot—that plague of wooden ships as Mr Grantham calls it in his recent publication—would be wholly avoided with iron—that there would be freedom from vermin, and from the stench and unhealthy consequences of bilge water.

'The directors were assured that the compasses could be easily adjusted; that with care oxidation could be guarded against, provided all parts of the ship should be examined or watched; that scarce a tithe of the expenditure required for keeping a wooden ship in repair was likely to ensue in iron; that, when necessary, repairs could be more quickly and easily effected; that there would be neither stripping of copper, sheathing, nor caulking; that nothing was to be apprehended from lightning, which in a wood-built ship is so frequently attended with fatal consequences—nor comparatively speaking from fire, one of its effects; that finer lines, with equal strength, were attainable, and, of course, greater speed; that they would not be so easily wrecked, whether striking on rock or beating over sand-banks; that they would run no risks from starting butts—were stiff under canvas; and that the only point where inferiority might be apprehended was in the fouling of the bottom, but that if means for providing against or removing this within the tropics, should prove incomplete, a steamer always rapidly progressing

while at sea, and whose ports will be in the high northern lati-
tudes of England and New York, where sea animalculae abound
but slightly, would have nothing to fear even on this point.

'An elaborate report setting forth these results of a most
laborious inquiry was laid before the board, and upon the
strength of it, but still more upon the recommendation of
Messrs Brunel and Guppy, the directors resolved to build their
ship of iron. Since this determination was acted upon, several
able pamphlets and papers have been published advocating iron
instead of wood for ship building; the best of which is that by
Mr Grantham of Liverpool with remarks by Messrs Fairbairn,
Creuse, and other eminent gentlemen. All are quite conclusive
in the most essential points as to the superiority of iron. The
directors had none of these lights to guide them; they placed
their confidence in their advisers and came to a decision upon
facts, and reasonings from facts, to which all that has since
been published has added nothing new, except the confirmative
results of practice while their Leviathan has been under the
hands of the mechanics.'

At the heart of the case against iron was the instinctive feeling
about its wrongness, preserved in this reply by an Admiralty
naval architect: 'Don't talk to me about iron ships, it's contrary
to nature.' Less hidebound opponents reasoned a little more—
iron ships would sink because of their weight, the engines would
make the iron vessel sag in the middle, or if it didn't the recipro-
cating machinery would cause the plate to fracture. The most
imaginative objection was that the sun shining on one side of
an iron ship would result in expansion and possibly fatal stresses
being set up. In some early experiments with cannon balls iron
plates were found to fracture on being hit, so a ban was put on
iron for Men of War and for contract mail ships—like the early
Cunarders—with a naval reserve commitment. This finding was
later reversed—iron ships suffered far less damage, and were
much more easily repaired when in action. There were two
valid objections to iron—first fouling; when HMS *Triton* came
back from a tour in the Mediterranean in 1846 she had a three-
inch coat of shell fish and coral on her iron bottom. The other
snag was the effect of iron on the compass which was an uncertain component in several disasters—including the grounding of the *Great Britain*—until the Liverpool Compass Committee thoroughly investigated the question with the help of

the *Great Britain*, and reported in 1860. During the 1840s iron became widely used for river craft where compasses did not count and fouling could be checked.

Convinced by Brunel's assessment of the theoretical advantages of iron, and Claxton's account of the material in practice, the GWSSCo approved its use. It continued to require only that the ship should be 2,000 tons burden. The Building Committee, which liked to keep its debates away from the ears of shareholders, explored the possibilities offered by iron during the winter of 1838-9. Immediately after the Board had decided to use iron, Captain Claxton wrote in a letter that her keel was to be 254 ft. long and she was to be not less than 40 ft. wide. A sketch of the midships section of the ship with this letter showed she was intended to be 'of the ordinary full shape'—her widest part would be below the waterline. Less than three months later, on 31 January 1839, another letter gives slightly larger dimensions with a keel length of 260 ft. and paddle shaft width of 41 ft. The diameter of the engine cylinders had gone up from $85\frac{1}{2}$ in. to 88 in., and was to jump to 100 in. by April. Finally, after making and rejecting four designs, the Building Committee agreed on the fifth plan for a vessel of 3,443 tons burden.

Whether tenders were invited for the job of building the ship is not clear. Paterson, whose yard made the *Great Western*, must have decided that he did not want the order. The size of the vessel indicated that it would be safer to build her in a dry dock so that probably worked out cheaper—even at £53,000, the price of the *Great Western*—for the GWSSCo to buy a piece of land and equip it themselves, having excavated the huge cradle for their creation. Both the company and Brunel appreciated the power of being able to make changes as they went along— much easier to do in your own yard.

In the absence of clear pointers to the steps by which the GWSSCo also became a shipbuilding firm, it is necessary to speculate. Paterson, though forward looking, was nervous of the revolutionary schemes in which Brunel specialised; it was Paterson who kept the *Great Western* some 500 tons smaller than Brunel had wanted on grounds of stability. With the vast new ship he probably felt that his yard might be so filled, and so altered, that more bread-and-butter lines would have to be abandoned. And, with a technical breakthrough on his stocks, how long would it be before the snags were ironed out and the mam-

moth floated away? As he was interested enough to stay on the
GWSSCo Design Committee, it is likely also, as has been
claimed, that he agreed to the use of his facilities and men.
When the switch to iron was made Paterson's facilities and the
experience of his men would have been less valuable. When in
1844 the yard was closing reference was made to 'mechanics
and other able hands, who are most of them strangers to Bristol'
being made redundant—so it looks as if the GWSSCo recruited
a labour force of its own, skilled in iron trades.

Doubts in the matter of the hull become certainties with the
engines. Nobody would put in a bid for making them because,
mainly, they were to be so big. Specifications were sent in
November 1838 to Maudslay, Son & Field at Lambeth, builders
of the *Great Western*'s engines, and to two other makers. Maudslay did not tender for the job and there was no response from
the other two. When, in April 1839, Brunel sought engines of
100-in. cylinder diameter and 7-ft. stroke, six manufacturers
were approached—Maudslay again, Hall, Seaward, Fawcett &
Preston, Bush, and Beddoes. Soon only Maudslay and Humphrys—Hall's designer—remained in competition for the order
with Brunel favouring Maudslay and urging what his enemies
said was impossible for him—a careful and unadventurous decision on the GWSSCo.

Humphrys put in the lowest bid with a maximum figure of
£30,700; Maudslay's tender was for £43,150 which included
bringing the engines to Bristol and installing them there.
Brunel's comment on Humphrys' bid was: 'Mr Humphrys is
over-sanguine, and the cost would greatly exceed the sum
named.' No allowance, he said, had been made for alterations,
waste, or damage 'which in a piece of machinery of this magni-
tude and novelty is bound to amount to a large sum'. The
GWSSCo directors twice sent back Humphrys' estimate for
further consideration because Brunel insisted that the work
could not be done that cheaply. Other postponements took place
so that Maudslay's could perfect a new twin-cylinder design
for paddle engines.

A company called Hall in Dartford had the manufacturing
rights for the 'trunk' engine patented by Humphrys. Its view
was that for such a large engine it would have to tool up with
equipment so big that they would never be used again which
would add disproportionately to the cost. It recommended the

GWSSCo to build its own engines. Inquiries in Bristol brought the news that factories there could not even produce the parts for the engine if these were to be sub-contracted out to them. So the steamship company decided to take Hall's advice and manufacture its own engines with the incentive that it could then become—as a profitable side-line—an engine maker and repairer for machinery on the scale required by the new generation of vessels of which the *Great Britain* would be the first example.

This last hope was frustrated when the shareholders got to hear about it. Some of them ran the plants that could not make the parts for the *Great Britain*'s engines, others were Bristol shipbuilders. They took legal advice which said that it would be out of order to use the capital of the GWSSCo for setting up an engine works to trade independently. The directors decided to press on with their own works, however, influenced chiefly by a report from Humphrys confirming the impossibility of getting his engines made in Bristol.

This decision—taken on 24 June 1839—went against Brunel's advice. He told the directors that the outlay would probably be greater in setting up their own works than in buying outside, in spite of the large savings Humphrys thought he could make. There was, therefore, a 'risk of the undertaking being too great for a newly formed establishment. The making of the vessel itself is no mean effort, and to superadd the construction of the largest pair of engines and boilers yet made, and upon a new plan, is calculating very much upon every effort being successful, and particularly of the continued assistance of those who have hitherto attended to the subject as it must be known to the directors that if Mr Guppy, for instance, should be prevented from giving his time as he has hitherto, or if Mr Humphrys should from illness or other causes leave us, the manufactory would be brought to a stand and the loss would be serious.

'I have no wish to deter the company from becoming their own manufacturers—I think it a course which must ultimately be adopted if the company thrive—but I should much prefer that it had been adopted gradually and that we had commenced with a vessel and then proceeded with boilers and repairs; and as our establishment became formed and matured and when we may no longer depend entirely upon the engineering talents and assistance of one director who may be unable to attend to it, or upon the health of one superintendent who as yet is alone in possession of all our plans and ideas, and at present is alone capable of carrying them out, we might then have ventured upon making the engines perhaps for a third vessel.'

In this letter, dated 12 June 1840, Brunel makes it clear that in comparing the tenders technically he considered them 'both excellently adapted to our particular case and the choice will depend upon other circumstances than the construction of the engines'.

In spite of this stated view that there was nothing to choose between the competing designs, it is clear that Brunel had reservations about Humphrys, if only on grounds of precarious health. He had good reasons for preferring to continue the connection with Maudslay. It was with the help of Henry Maudslay, then working in small premises off Oxford Street, London, that Brunel's father, Marc, had set up the plant in which he revolutionised the production of blocks for use with the ropes and sails of warships. This association, started at the turn of the nineteenth century, continued, and Brunel wrote in a letter to Henry Maudslay's son about 'your firm, with which all my early recollections of engineering are so closely connected, and in whose manufactory I probably acquired all my early knowledge of mechanics'. Added to this Guppy had himself been apprenticed at Maudslay's Lambeth works. So if in all these new and vast proposals there is a leaning towards an old and friendly firm by the GWSSCo's engineers the reason was understandable.

As makers of excellent machines, Maudslay, Son & Field was also slower than Brunel liked in producing the goods, and tended to be conservative. The proposal for building the engines 'at home' went ahead and, once decided, the plant was quickly set up. But problems continued to arise because of the great size of the engines and on 24 November 1839 Francis Humphrys wrote a letter which alone brings him a little reflected immortality from the enterprise. Its result has until very recently been far better remembered than the entire *Great Britain* project in which, paradoxically, it took no part—James Nasmyth's steam hammer. Hearing on the *Great Western* grape-vine that Nasmyth had built 20 highly commended locomotives for the Great Western Railway, Humphrys wrote to him about the paddle shaft.

'I find that there is not a forge hammer in England or Scotland powerful enough to forge the intermediate paddle shaft of the engines for the *Great Britain*. What am I to do? Do you think I might dare to use cast iron?'

Looking back from the 1880s Nasmyth, another of Maudslay's pupils, wrote: 'This letter set me a-thinking. How was it that the existing hammers were incapable of forging a wrought iron shaft of 30 inches diameter? Simply because of their want of compass, of range and fall, as well as of their want of power of blow.

'A few moments rapid thought satisfied me that it was by our rigidly adhering to the old traditional form of a smith's hand hammer, of which the forge and tilt hammer, although driven by water or steam power were mere enlarged modifications, that the difficulty had arisen, as when the largest forge hammer was tilted up to its full height its range was so small that when a piece of work of considerable size was placed on the anvil, the hammer became "gagged" so that when the forging required the most powerful blow it received next to no blow at all, as the clear space for the fall of the hammer was almost entirely occupied by the work on the anvil.... In a little more than half an hour after receiving Mr Humphrys' letter narrating his unlooked for difficulty I had the whole contrivance in all its executant details before me in a page of my scheme book.... Mr Humphrys was delighted with my design.'

Half an hour's inspired doodling gave to engineers a major opportunity to enlarge the scale of their designs. While this was going on Brunel was devoting thought independently to the engines. He sent Berkeley Claxton, Captain Claxton's son, on six trips in the *Great Western* to measure the extent of roll and pitch, and the exact performance of the engines. The end of it was that he preferred the screw propeller.

'The engines which Mr Humphrys had so elaborately designed, and which were far advanced in construction were given up to his inexpressible regret and mortification, as he had pinned his hopes as a practical engineer on the results of their performance,' wrote Nasmyth. 'And to crown his distress he was ordered to produce fresh designs of engines especially suited for screw propulsion.

'Mr Humphrys was a man of the most sensitive and sanguine constitution of mind. The labour and anxiety which he had already undergone, and perhaps the disappointment of his hopes, proved too much for him and a brain fever carried him off after a few days illness.'

This caused a reshuffle in the organisation. A Mr Harman was made assistant engineer under Thomas Guppy who, on Brunel's recommendation, was put in command of the works, and left his seat on the Board.

Brunel's anxieties about Humphrys' health assume a malign quality in the light of his early death. No note of regret appears from anybody except Nasmyth. Brunel's son, in his biography of his father, bypasses the incident in the evasive compression 'Mr Humphrys resigned'. A sad business. Guppy was much more to Brunel's liking. He had been the leading figure in the group which founded the GWR, was much travelled and diverse in his interests, and he supported Brunel's novel ideas. He was altogether more robust than his predecessor, being the first man publicly to indulge in a dangerous sport, still occasionally practised. He walked on the roofs of train carriages on the way back from a lunch inaugurating a new stretch of the GWR in 1838. He settled in Naples in 1849, founded a big engineering business, and died there in 1882.

Changing from wood to iron in the building of their ship was momentous enough. To alter the propulsion system at a stage when the hull had been designed for paddles was an act of faith that Brunel, alone among engineers, was able to persuade a board to make. With Cunard coming on fast, and competing with the *British Queen*, the *Great Western*'s receipts were threatened. Having gone far beyond the point of making two or three more *Great Westerns*, the GWSSCo was now irrevocably committed by its investment to a form of 'secret weapon' policy for the transatlantic ferry war: a ship that in size, style, speed, comfort, and novelty would amaze the travelling public and never leave port with an empty berth.

This is not to suggest that the GWSSCo was, at this stage anyway, run by a group of desperate men seeking for an escape in any gimmick that came to hand. The adoption of the propeller was a considered decision. The steps towards it began when the propeller-driven three-masted schooner *Archimedes* came to Bristol at the end of May 1840. She had been launched in November 1838 by the Ship Propeller Company as a vehicle for testing the propeller invented by Francis Pettit Smith, a farmer originally from Hythe in Kent who had nurtured a belief in propellers by experiments with model boats. The *Archimedes* had made trips to the Continent, and been extensively shown to the Royal Navy. With a speed of nine knots she had created a favourable impression everywhere, as the first 'man-sized' (237 tons) ship in the world driven by a propeller.

When she came to Bristol some of the GWSSCo directors went for a trip in her, and Guppy, who was with them, asked Mr Smith and Captain E. Chappell RN (an Admiralty observer) if he could make the proposed voyage to Liverpool on board.

'On the passage enough rough weather was encountered to show,' said Guppy, 'that the screw possessed several good points, and was not so absolutely impracticable as had been asserted.'

Although not completely swayed, Guppy suggested that work on the *Great Britain*—particularly with the engines and that part of the hull affected by the paddle equipment—should be suspended for three months. This was agreed and Brunel was called on to make a report. So were Claxton, Humphrys, and Paterson whose opinions against any change from paddles was submitted to Brunel.

The *Archimedes* was hired for six months from the Propeller Company while Brunel, helped by Guppy and Captain Claxton carried out tests with her. Berkeley Claxton was sent on one of his 'voyages of observation' to Oporto. On 10 October 1840 Brunel presented a report which favoured the propeller and altered the course of technical history.

He begins by saying that 'the *Archimedes* has proved in a satisfactory and undeniable manner that a screw acting against the water with a surface even much smaller than that offered by the paddle boards of a well-proportioned paddle wheel will propel the ship at a very fair speed, but at what expense of power this effect has been produced is not so evident'. A major loss of power—sometimes as much as a third—occurs through paddles slipping as the water yields. The ratio of the area of the surface of the *Archimedes* propeller (26 sq. ft.) to the area of the midships section of the vessel (about 122 sq. ft.) was 1 to 4.7 while the ratio of propelling area to midships section in the *Great Western* was 1 to 2.56.

As an index of wasted effort Brunel compared the distance travelled by screw and paddle with the distance covered by the ship they were respectively driving. The *Great Western* moved

forward one unit while her paddles travelled through 1.27 units
—slightly better than the *Archimedes* where the ratio was 1 to
1.29. Some paddlers, however, showed ratios of over 1 to 1.5.
From these figures he deduced that the propeller, if it presented
the same area to the water, could expect to 'slip as little or less
than the ordinary paddle boards'.

This conclusion struck at a major contemporary misconcep-
tion about the propeller: 'There is a great mistake committed
in assuming that the action of the screw is a very oblique action
tending rather to drive the water laterally with a rotary motion
than to push it steadily backwards ... the mass of water pushed
backwards by the action of the screw appears to be very large
... it is forgotten that the screw is moving forward with the
ship, and therefore that the angle at which the water is struck
by the plane is diminished by all that much that the ship with
the screw advances.'

Continuing to use the *Great Western* as a yardstick, Brunel
considered the amount of power used by the *Archimedes* to
achieve her 8⅓ knots. 'Comparing this with the gross power of
the *Great Western* engines when propelling that vessel at the
same velocity with the advantage of better lines, and the other
advantages arising from greater dimensions—there does not
appear any such discrepancy as to indicate any loss of power
with the use of the screw in the *Archimedes*. On the contrary—
the power expended in the *Great Western* is actually as great as
that in the *Archimedes* as compared with their relative midship
sections, and if any great allowance is to be made for the circumstances which I have referred to of longer dimensions and better
lines there would appear to be actually less power expended in
proportion to the dimensions and form of the *Archimedes* than
in the *Great Western*.'

After commenting on the effects of friction Brunel concluded
'that as compared with the ordinary paddle wheel of seagoing
steamers the screw is, both as regards the effect produced, and
the proportion of power required to obtain that effect, an
inefficient propeller'.

What possible snags argued against using a propeller in the
Great Britain? Brunel dealt with four; first the need for 'a
peculiar form of vessel'. On this he said 'a clean run is the most
essential condition and I should suppose no ship was ever built
in which this principle of form was carried to a greater extent

than in our new Iron Ship. Secondly, the propeller would be inaccessible, and liable to be damaged on going aground—'This appears to me the objection most plausible,' wrote Brunel, but said the propeller could be stopped at any time and shaft bearings examined, and in port divers could examine for damage or entanglements. There was no chance of injuring the propeller on going aground if it was, as his model showed, above the line of the keel.

Mr Berkeley Claxton's long spells afloat with a notebook added confidence to Brunel's answer to the next disadvantage—that the pitching of the ship would often throw the propeller clear of the water. Though uncertain quite why, Brunel said that the stern of a ship seldom cleared the surface—a mark of nine feet on the stern of the *Great Western* was the lowest ever seen and that 'rarely and only for very short intervals'.

Lastly, Brunel dealt with the question of effectively driving the propeller. 'Upon this point certainly the *Archimedes* offers but a miserable example, and the result is almost enough to prejudice the mind of any person against the whole scheme. The proportions as I have before stated of the gearing are so bad that the engines appear even to the eye to labour ineffectually to get up their speed. The required speed of the screw is not nearly attained while the noise and tremor caused by the machinery is such as to render the vessel uninhabitable and perfectly unfit for passengers, I should almost say for crew....

'The most simple and effectual means of overcoming all objections on these heads always appeared to me to be by the use of straps instead of gearing. I have seen a great deal of the working of machinery by straps and ropes in the numerous works executed by my father, and all my experience leads me to the conclusion that there existed no difficulty whatever in sending the necessary power through a rope or a hemp strap.'

Use of the screw would, on the other hand, bring important gains to the *Great Britain*. It would save 95 tons in weight compared with paddles, and 160 tons of engine weight would be shifted from paddle shaft level, ten feet above the waterline, to seven feet below it with consequent benefits to the vessel's stability and safety. In his description of the next asset to be gained from the propeller, Brunel gives a clue to the possible reason why the *Great Britain* grew too wide to get out of Bristol docks.

A propeller allowed for a simpler form of ship. 'The almost infinite resources afforded by the material enabled us to expand the sides and obtain breadth of beam for capital cabin room both before and abaft the paddles, and contract the sides at the paddles as seen upon the plan, but in order to strengthen this part, so evidently weak by form, much contrivance and much material was required. By dispensing with paddles the best form of ship is left free to be adopted, perfect lines may be preserved, more equal strength obtained with increased space, and the whole mass of paddle boxes and their accompanying sponsons and deck houses swept away and the resistance of these large wings to headwinds or seas entirely avoided. The space gained by avoiding the contraction is calculated by Mr Paterson to amount to 200 tons measurement.'

According to Captain Hosken on the *Great Western*, when the paddles were deeply immersed the engine used two thirds of its power driving unproductively against the resistance of the water—the propeller would work just as well deep, shallow or 'as long as it be immersed, if the vessel were on her beam ends, or bottom upwards'. Deeply-buried paddles also reduced the usefulness of sails—with a propeller sails could be used at any time and the propeller could be disconnected to prevent its drag slowing the ship down. Variations in the degree of depth of paddle wheels often meant, in bad weather, that a plunge at one moment almost stopped the engines, and at the next both wheels left the water and the engines raced causing great alarm and some damage.

At the very start of the screw propeller there was a belief—especially in the Royal Navy—that having the propulsion at the stern would somehow make the steering unreliable and allow the ship to drift about largely out of control. Brunel pointed out that the propeller pushing water past the rudder enhanced steering to the extent of giving a captain control over a ship even when he was not moving. The final advantage was a local one—the *Great Britain* would have been 78 ft. wide as a paddle steamer; now she would be 'under 50 ft.'.

At the end of his 8,000 word report Brunel wrote: 'From all that I have said it must be evident to you Gentlemen that my opinion is strong and decided in favour of the advantage of employing the screw in the new ship—it certainly is so. I am fully aware of the responsibilities I take upon myself by giving this advice. I am also fully sensible of the large amount we have at stake and I have not forgotten the nature and the tone of the observations which have on more occasions than one been so freely made by individuals upon the course we have hitherto pursued although, and I have pleasure in referring to the fact, this course has, in every instance the results have been obtained, been successful to us. But my conviction of the wisdom, I may almost say the necessity, of our adopting the improvement I now recommend is so strong and I feel it is too well founded for me to hesitate or shrink from the responsibility.'

With this last and largest change approved the Iron Ship—whose name was altered speculatively from *City of New York*, through *Mammoth*, to *Great Britain* while she was building—sank into relative obscurity. She continued to be a shrine for technical pilgrimage for, as Captain Claxton records: 'The sides of the *Great Britain* were scarcely visible over the walls of the yard in which she was building when naval officers, ship-builders, engineers, and philosophers from all countries began to seek admittance, and many have been the papers which in most languages have been written on the comparative merits of iron and wood as a material for ship building which would not probably have seen the light had not a scale of dimensions been decided upon which may create astonishment at the present moment, but will probably excite no more wonder in a few years than the size of the *Great Western* does at present.'

There were no upheavals during the next two years. In the background the GWSSCo became progressively more anxious about the financial state of its concern as Cunard engrossed more and more of the traffic which was expanding at the rate (Cunard estimated) of ten per cent a year. A result of this was, as the notes for Isambard's biography of his father say, that 'the completion of the *Great Britain* was delayed many months owing to the financial condition of the company which had been seriously affected by competition'.

Work went ahead along the lines Brunel indicated; the stern of the ship was altered to take the propeller and shaft—at a cost estimated by Brunel at £200. The engines—impossible now that the screw was adopted for them to be any other than 'home made'—came out finally rather like the original Maudslay tender (which had been for four cylinders of maximum diameter 77¾ in.). Guppy and Brunel made an inverted four-cylinder engine with diameters of 88 in., increased by 8 in. over the first plan. This engine was only a paddle engine turned longways and fitted with a large drum geared up, like a bicycle, to a small drum attached to the propeller shaft. It worked at only four to five pounds per square inch steam pressure.

While construction went on smoothly if intermittently at Bristol, Brunel began for the first time to have dealings with the Admiralty. The Navy's leaders had asked for a copy of the October 1840 report on the propeller. An interview followed on 27 April 1841. This formed the beginning of an anti-Government story Brunel afterwards took relish in telling. 'I attended the board. Lord Minto (then first Lord) stated that he wished a complete experiment to be made on the applicability of the screw to Government boats and he proposed to place the conduct of the experiments in my hands. As a professional man I stated that I should take great pleasure in doing it and take great interest in it provided they intended to make a good experiment and would place it entirely in my hands without the intervention of any Government office.'

Brunel was to report directly to the Board, and to be entirely his own master—Lord Minto 'took me apart to the window to express this last condition'. From the way the story is recorded the initiative for this meeting came from the Admiralty. Doubtless this was so. But Brunel had good reason for welcoming the chance to test his conclusions about the propeller, and about the engine that would drive it best.

'For several successive years,' according to Captain Claxton, 'hopes were entertained that the experiments in the *Rattler* would enable the engineers of the *Great Britain* to arrive at the best conclusions, both as to the number of arms, and the best pitch of the screw: but the ship progressing towards completion, and the *Rattler* not appearing in the field, Mr Brunel was urged by the Directors to come to some decision in order that a screw might be put in hand, and the one now adopted is the result. As far as it has been tried, it is an excellent propeller: but there is no doubt that a little more delay would have produced one of fewer arms and more pitch; and still better results may be expected from the spare screw which has been ordered.'

With the Admiralty's commission so particularly and exclusively given him, Brunel went ahead and ordered a 200-horsepower twin-cylinder engine from Maudslay. When it was nearly finished he began making inquiries about the ship into which it would be fitted—a ship with a carrying capacity of 800 tons had been agreed. 'Nowhere could she be found,' records Brunel's son. 'Minutes were searched at the Admiralty and it was ascertained that the ship was ordered and that was all. No ship was laid down. There was of course considerable surprise excited at this discovery and shortly afterwards Brunel was sent for to the Admiralty to wait upon Sir George Cockburn.' He was the new First Lord.

Sir George got to the point at once. 'Do you mean to suppose that we shall cut up Her Majesty's ships after this fashion, sir?' he said handing Brunel a model of the stern of an old-fashioned three-decker of the *Dreadnought* hospital ship class out of which large slices had been taken to make room for the screw, exposing the whole of the lower deck 'so as to make the application of the screw look very ridiculous'. On this exhibit was written 'Mr Brunel's mode of applying the screw to Her Majesty's ships'.

Brunel said he'd never seen it before. Sir George said: 'Why sir you sent it to the Admiralty.' Brunel said he hadn't. Sir George rang the bell and asked where the model had come from, and while waiting for the answer Brunel scraped off the model's inscription with his pen-knife. The reply was that the model had come from the Surveyor's office. The Surveyor, Sir William Symonds, was a pathological opponent of steam, iron, propellers, and progress.

In his diary Sir William (Surveyor from 1832 to 1847) refers to the new vessels as 'monstrous *iron* steamers'. When more were on order he issued warnings: 'I spoke plainly of the risk to Sir George Cockburn and foretold their fate. He replied "Pooh, pooh, pooh".' When his colleagues stopped listening Sir William pulled up the drawbridge at the Surveyor's office—where the Navy's vessels were designed—'there was then scarcely any communication between the Surveyor's office and the new Engineering Dept which for some time continued to act independently of it'. Commented Sir William's biographer, 'In building a steamer all that was done by one dept was to allow so much space for the engines to be provided by the other, and important alterations might be subsequently carried out in a vessel without the necessary correspondence between the two. Many blunders resulted from this absurd arrangement.'

This extraordinary man's influence extended even to an innocent experiment which Brunel wanted to try with the *Polyphemus*, an RN paddler, at Southampton, relating the power output to the speed achieved. A measured mile was to have been marked, but wasn't. So the ever unassuming Captain Claxton spent more than three hours stumbling about in the low-tide mud measuring off a statute and a nautical mile. Sir William Symonds arrived next day, and, a memoir recalls: 'Great was his surprise....'

There being no special ship to put Maudslay's engine into, the Admiralty offered the *Acheron* but Brunel said that it was wholly the wrong shape, and that its full stern could not take a propeller. Hearing no more he resigned and was at once summoned back to the Admiralty where, making no reference at all to what had passed, the Lords told him—as if he were a fractious child—that his propeller was to be tried first. Brunel said that he was not a competitor but an arbiter which provoked 'tedious fencing' before all was agreed.

The *Rattler*, 888 tons burden, 179 ft. 6 in. long by 32 ft. 8½ in. wide, already being built as a paddler, was to be adapted to take a propeller. It was built at Sheerness (though no amount of asking would reveal this) and launched on 13 April 1843 and delivered to Maudslay's in 'the roughest possible condition'. Sir William's ministrations ensured she had no copper plating and was daubed only in lumpy tar. That the gap of two years between the first Admiralty approach to Brunel and the launching of the *Rattler* is not fuller of pleadings and recriminations may be because Brunel suffered from debility resulting from overwork. This is the conclusion of L. T. C. Rolt—on what he admits is slight evidence—in his biography. It might be an additional reason, too, for apparent tranquillity at the Great Western Dock in Bristol.

He was back on bristling good form by 15 September 1843 in a letter to Field with whom, in any business with Maudslay, Son & Field, he usually dealt. 'After you left me this morning I looked back to a few dates and memoranda to see the rate at which the works on the *Rattler* had progressed—I should rather say the periods during which they have stood still. It really is most distressing to think of—the force of example seems to have been irresistible. The vessel was tediously slow in being made, and you have caught the complaint. Let me beg you as a personal favour that you will exert yourselves a little. I dare say, indeed I know, that much of this delay is attributed by many to me. I do not believe one day has been lost through me from the commencement and if blame—which is richly deserved somewhere—should be openly thrown upon me, I shall be obliged to cast it off on the right shoulder, and I much fear that you cannot escape altogether.

'I must seriously urge you to a little more exertion and as a mere matter of business, depend upon it you are wrong. These are moving days when pushing forward is much safer than holding back; and you may find with the screw, as with the direct engines, that it is better to be ahead of your neighbours. You must remember what a very deaf ear you turned to me when I so strongly urged direct engines upon you for the *Great Western*. Nothing but beams would satisfy your conservative notions—do not run the risk of quarrelling with screws, they may also turn out good things.'

With this prophetic hope in his heart Brunel started the *Rattler* experiments on 30 October 1843—more than three months after the *Great Britain* had been launched and started her fitting out. They went on until the end of the following April. At the start the *Rattler* could manage only 5 knots and 6 furlongs at full power and 18 r.p.m.; by April $9\frac{1}{2}$ knots had been achieved. Brunel thought that further alterations with the propeller would take them over 10 knots but after that the engine's limited power would become critical.

Uncharacteristically Brunel does not seem to have been much wiser at the end of the six-month *Rattler* trials than he was at the beginning. When he saw the *Archimedes*, and made tests on her, he went away and produced his paper. At the end of the *Rattler* trials he did not produce a paper outlining the theoretical basis on which the best size and shape of propeller could be worked out. He had not expected to. His 1840 report said that a theoretical assessment 'involves much more complicated calculations than have generally been applied, and would indeed require that which we hardly possess'. The Wright brothers making their aeroplane were astonished to find at the turn of the present century that what they thought would be the easy bit— the propeller—was still a subject without solid theoretical foundation which they began to provide. Brunel may, perhaps, be excused.

However, doing it the slow way with the tests on the Thames

made a well-planned work programme difficult in Bristol. A two-bladed propeller was used to start with, then a three—then a four-bladed example. Maudslay's was peppered with orders as screws broke in action; to speed production Brunel said he would take propeller arms cast in brass with separately-made blades attached later. From letters it appears that the diameters of the experimental propellers went down as did the number of blades. Then in mid-March larger diameters returned to favour and ways of altering the stern of the ship to get 'another inch of radius' were sought. Worried about loss of power through giving the water near the root of the propeller blade circular movement Brunel wanted to reduce the length (i.e., along the axis of the shaft) of the blade. This weakened the blade.

In Guppy's office the outcome of the tests was a sequence of notes. On 23 October 1843: 'I should wish, therefore, that the GWSSCo would go to the expense to make one as follows, diameter 9 feet 9 inches, four armed, the pitch of the blades up to 5 feet 9 inches diameter to be 9 feet 8 inches and to change quickly so as at 6 feet 6 inches diameter to be 11 feet 2 inches pitch ... let it be a very good casting and rubber smooth. I believe our large one must have a similar change in the pitch.'

On 27 November 1843: 'A chance word in your note—"your screw"—makes me recollect that it very likely might be called *my screw* and this makes me pause and request you to pause before doing anything till I have thought again.' On 6 February 1844: 'In bending the arms of the screw to the right shape you will leave the roots and alter the ends only. I do not remember the point at which it was determined to commence the altered pitch but I think now—with some further experience on the *Rattler*—that if 4 feet radius or 8 feet diameter of the centre part is at the reduced pitch, it will give nine inches for the transition. Then at 4 feet 9 inches radius or 9 feet 6 inches diameter it will be at the increased pitch. The greatest bends will then only be about 1¼ inches.'

On 13 February 1844: 'Have you set any of the arms of the screw? If not I must correct the dimension I gave—I think the pitch had better vary at 3 feet to 4 feet instead of 4 feet 9 inches. I hope this is in time as some late experiments lead me to attach importance to it. The centre part may have a pitch as small as 22 inches if in bending you find it easy.'

Finally in a letter to the Admiralty Brunel explains that a

late refinement 'consists in making the centre part of the screw of considerably less pitch than the exterior, with a view of diminishing the rotatory motion given to the water. This modification has been adopted by me in the construction of the screw for the *Great Britain*. I think it likely to produce a good effect.'

Experience with a multi-belt drive from a bigger to a smaller drum in the *Rattler* weaned Brunel away from his belief that this kind of transmission—used successfully by his father—was appropriate to the very high-powered, non-stop applications in marine engineering. Responding perhaps to raised eyebrows at the start of the *Rattler* trials, he said: 'The use of the straps in this vessel is merely a temporary contrivance for the purpose of experimenting upon the screw and adjusting the number of revolutions to that which shall be ascertained by actual trial to be the most effective—trials which could not be made with cog wheels. That the use of straps with so large a power being unusual it may require some attention and probably some alterations....' He sought advice from Maudslay: 'The straps should be well softened with oil' ... and again he said, strangely for a friction drive: 'I believe you will find that the straps will take a great deal of oil.'

The mechanism worked well enough for Brunel to record on 5 February 1844 that there was 'no perceptible slip of the straps' at 9¼ knots. On 3rd April 1845, the *Rattler* took part in the famous test with the paddler *Alecto* in which the vessels were tied stern to stern for a tug of war. The *Rattler*, using a two-bladed Smith propeller, won by dragging the *Alecto* astern at 2.8 knots. This, added to the great vulnerability of paddles in action, brought the Admiralty finally to favour the propeller. But not Sir William Symonds, of course, whose biographer notes that 'having at this date only the performance of the *Rattler* before him, Sir William was inclined to doubt the efficiency of this propeller for general purposes'.

Delays with the *Rattler* trials meant that the GWSSCo had to go ahead with Brunel's first propeller—six blades of wrought iron 15 ft. 6 in. in diameter weighing three tons seventeen hundredweight with a pitch of 25 ft. This was replaced—it disintegrated—after the first season on the Atlantic with a four-bladed propeller much more robust and without 'palms' riveted on the ends of the arms. At seven tons, it was almost twice as heavy as its predecessor.

There was little to complain about with the six-bladed propeller when the *Great Britain* set off on her first trial on 12 December 1844, the day after her first and last departure from Bristol docks. Steam was raised as she was towed down the Avon from her overnight mudbank and a trip of several hours undertaken. A top speed of 11 knots was recorded. The next trial was on 8 January 1845 when a large party of shareholders was to be shown, along with some scientists and engineers, what the *Great Britain* could do—for some hours the answer was 'nothing' because of dense fog. The pilot at last allowed a short run to be made during which 11½ knots was recorded. On 20 January the *Great Britain* was taken to Ilfracombe and back, 95 nautical miles altogether, which she did in eight and a half hours averaging 11 knots.

With these creditable—but hardly exhaustive—tests behind her, the GWSSCo decided to send its ship to London. She would earn more money there as an exhibit than she would by being put straight on the Atlantic station in mid-winter when traffic almost disappeared. Exposure in the Thames would show that the enormous ship did exist, had been launched, and could sail. It would be a useful way of advertising the company and attracting future customers.

She set off into the beginnings of a gale on the evening of 23 January. The next morning it was blowing a gale and at 3.20 in the afternoon the *Great Britain* was hit by a heavy sea on the starboard bow which, says the log, 'drove in three 7 inch portlights, and did some other slight damage to the upper works'. It is thought that the best-known print of the ship during this part of her life is a reconstruction of the impact of that 3.20 p.m. wave. The ship scarcely wavered, rounded the Lizard into fine weather and reached Blackwall, London, in 59½ hours giving an average speed, as Thomas Guppy recorded it, of 'upwards of 9½ knots, and if allowance be made for times, when, on account of the bearings becoming warm, the engines went slowly, the average speed may fairly be reckoned at 10 knots'.

Ten knots seems to these steamship pioneers to have had the same magic quality as 100 miles an hour for ton-up kids now. Guppy was upset not to have achieved it. 'Owing to the inefficiency of the stokers, the steam was not regularly or well kept

up, and the pressure varied from 2 p.s.i. to 5 p.s.i., being frequently low ... the crew of sailors consisted chiefly of that
indifferent class usually shipped for short runs, to whom of
course the rig of the ship was perfectly new. Some of the engineers stood well to their duty, but others, and nearly all the
stokers, were completely knocked up with sea-sickness.'

On this first trip the *Great Britain* revealed a characteristic
she was to retain—a tendency to roll. Guppy conceded 'considerable' rolling—but blamed 40 tons of chains on deck and
high-stowed coal for raising her centre of gravity. But if the
rolling was uncomfortable, Brunel was correct in saying that
she would never pitch enough to expose the propeller—Guppy
said it never came more than half out of the water causing
slight engine acceleration 'during perhaps half a revolution'.

Brunel, advising a friend about the arrival of his ship in
London, accompanied the directions with an engaging—and apt
—picture. 'She will, if all goes right, be in the Thames on Sunday morning the 26th, and I think it not at all impossible that
we may some early day lower masts and come up river as
Gulliver walked through the streets of Lilliput with his coat tails
tucked up.'

Captain Hosken, in command, matched this exuberant hope
by approaching the Thames that Sunday lunchtime against a
very strong gale at about nine knots noting 'Gravesend reach
full of vessels—steered in and out between them at full speed.
Ran the measured knot in six minutes 16 seconds, going 16
r.p.m.' The *Great Britain* moored at Blackwall at 3.30 p.m. The
only casualty on this voyage was the bowsprit of a collier brig
that drifted into the iron ship as she waltzed up the Thames.

The stay in London was a success. Crowds turned out to see
her arrive and came to see over her in their thousands. On 15
April Queen Victoria set out with a large retinue over Vauxhall
Bridge via Camberwell and Peckham for Greenwich where she
got into the royal steam tender *Dwarf* for the last part of the
trip. From this point she was accompanied by the Lord Mayor
of London proceeding ahead with his entourage in the state
barge. Presumably for the sake of keeping up to the modern
mark the barge was towed by a steam tug. The royal party,
which included Prince Albert, was all amazement as well they
might be because the *Great Britain* was fully 500 tons larger
than anything up to then built and more than one third (322 ft.

to 210 ft.) longer than the largest man-of-war with 120 guns.

The Queen went to the stern and looked forward, and then went to the raised forecastle and looked aft. The engines were seen and Brunel operated a working model of them showing how they could be reversed. Mr F. P. Smith gave the Queen a model of the propeller he had just designed for her new yacht tender, *Fairy*, and models were shown of the *Great Britain*'s six-bladed propeller, the four-bladed reserve propeller, and of a three-bladed propeller which was presumably the most up-to-date embodiment of the results of the *Rattler* trials.

Captain Hosken was given the job of escorting the Queen and he recalled, years later, an arch little incident: 'As Her Majesty was going down to the engine room, she appeared a little nervous and asked if she was near the bottom. I told her there was only one step more and offered her my hand as to any other lady without a thought of etiquette, and the queen received it quite simply. Some who were present remarked, "Hosken has put his foot in it, he ought to have offered his arm, not his hand".' How near was Hosken then to a knighthood, one wonders, with 64 transatlantic passages behind him as master of the *Great Western*, and now succeeding to the command of this great new vessel?

Gilded by royal visit, and with the fine weather approaching, the natural thing to hear of next would be a bustle of activity to get the *Great Britain* on her station and earning revenue. In this spirit Prince Albert asked Captain Hosken on 15 April when the voyages would begin, to which he got the answer that the plan was to start at the end of July or the first weeks in August. The prince supposed that Captain Hosken wished to save the equinox and was told, enigmatically, that the point was to make one or two voyages as speedily as possible to convince the public that the *Great Britain* was completely safe.

There is no record of any work being done in the Thames to make more certain of her safety and reliability. Possibly the GWSSCo hoped it would be made an offer for the ship—the directors had been told by the shareholders 'in the strongest manner' to get rid of the works at Bristol, and the *Great Western*. This would not only provide funds to finish the *Great Britain*, said a company report of late 1844, but be 'a step preparatory to the disposal of that ship when completed and the final dissolution of the company'.

It was proposed to that November meeting that the company should try to raise another £50,000 in capital, which with Cunard burgeoning on his mail subsidy and an American line of steamers promised, would not have been easy to do. Perhaps the likeliest reason for this hiatus is that there was not enough money in the petty cash even to stock the ship, pay the crew, and keep the engines turning on Atlantic voyages where a full pay load was uncertain.

On 12 June the *Great Britain* left the Thames for a leisurely exhibition cruise, stayed a few days in Plymouth, then went to Dublin before returning to Liverpool. On the way back across the Irish Sea one of the four engine cylinders 'gave out' and the voyage was completed on two of the remaining three. In Dublin, as in London, many thousands paid to view the ship, bringing in some easy revenue—but it would have taken more than 400,000 visitors at a shilling a head to match the annual revenue of £22,465 which the GWSSCo directors expected the *Great Britain* to earn.

Only once in this account of the *Great Britain* does Brunel refer to any of his other commitments. It may appear for this reason that the building of the *Great Britain*, and coping with its subsequent problems, was a full-time job. Indeed it may have been a full-time job. Brunel was, however, busy with a lot of other full-time jobs. Over the Christmas before the GWSSCo was founded he calculated that he had in hand work to the value of £5,590,000 comprising chiefly the Great Western Railway, but also five other railways, two docks, and two bridges. 'A pretty considerable capital at the age of 29,' he reflected.

During the whole of the creative period at the GWSSCo— until well into 1841—Brunel's main preoccupation was with the GWR in whose interest he raced about the West Country in his 'Flying Hearse', the self-designed mobile office and rest room drawn by four horses. The main London–Bristol stretch of the line opened in June 1841. From 1838 Brunel's 7-ft. broad gauge was under attack by what was known as the 'Liverpool Party' among the GWR shareholders. There is a suggestion that their correct conviction about the error of broad gauge, and the fierce campaign they fought and nearly won against it, was intensified by Brunel's flanking threat through the *Great Western* and *Great Britain* to Liverpool's rising status as a port.

In July 1844 the South Devon Railway was approved by Parliament which was the beginning of the atmospheric railway experiment in which Brunel applied the electric railway principle before electricity had been sufficiently developed. And just as the *Great Britain* was due to set out on her maiden voyage in July 1845, the Royal Commission on Railway Gauges started its inquiries. During the whole GWSSCo period there was almost non-stop Parliamentary business before committees evaluating railway proposals; and in offering F. P. Smith an additional idea for his propeller Brunel talked of 'these patenting days'. Although in another letter he wrote: 'I assure you my dear sir that in the present active busy times it is very difficult to invent anything new,' many tried, and there was a ferment in law courts and out of them of patent claim and counter-claim.

For those 50 or so passengers who bought a ticket for the first Atlantic crossing there was plenty to distract their minds from apprehensions about the novelty of the vessel. More than a third of the space was devoted to engines and coal bunkers. Something like another third was for passengers' use, divided into two sections before and aft of the engines. Each of these areas was on two levels, the one immediately below the main deck was a promenade some 30 ft. wide, and below that was the dining saloon functionally laid out like an army cookhouse (or Oxbridge college hall). Around the perimeter of these central open spaces, lit by skylights from the main deck like gardeners' cold frames which were duplicated on the promenade decks to carry the light down to the dining saloons—around these were the cabins. They were set out in blocks of four, each one about 6 ft. 3 in. long and containing an upper and lower berth—much the sort of dimension in a British Railways sleeper now. On each side of the after saloon—basically the one for first class passengers— was a group of rooms for ladies only with access to a boudoir, and to the stewardesses' cabins, without going into the public corridor.

Extracts from an American description show that the GWSSCo inaugurated with diffidence interior decor in steamers which its successors elaborated later to assault the sensibilities of travellers. 'The walls of the after saloon are painted in delicate tints. A row of well-proportioned pillars which range down the centre of the promenade serve the double purpose of ornament to the room and support to the deck. The framework of the staircases is of iron; the stairs are far more wide and commodious than is generally met with on ship-board. From this promenade you descend into the main or dining saloon which is 98 ft. 6 in. long and 30 ft. wide.

'This is really a beautiful room. A large sum of money has not been uselessly squandered in procuring for it gaudy decoration, not harmonizing with its uses, but its fittings are alike chaste and elegant. Down the centre are twelve principal columns of white and gold with ornamental capitals of great beauty. Twelve similar columns also range down the walls on either side. Between these latter and the entrances to the sleeping berths are eight pilasters in the Arabesque style (of which character the saloon generally partakes) beautifully painted with oriental birds and flowers. The archways of the several doors are tastefully carved and gilded and are surmounted with neat medallion heads. Some looking-glasses are so arranged as to reflect the saloon lengthways at two opposite sides from which a very pleasing illusion is produced. The walls of this apartment are of a delicate lemon tinted drab hue, relieved with blue, white, and gold. At the stern end are a number of sofas which range one above the other nearly to the stern lights.' The captain had a cabin near the ladies' boudoir, and the officers had quarters on the upper deck, the crew in the lower deck, of the forecastle.

With 600 tons of cargo compensating partly for the few passengers—she had room for 360—the *Great Britain* sailed for America from Liverpool on 26 July 1845. Little survives, under the eaves of the razzamatazz of her arrival in New York on 10 August, about the momentous voyage itself. It is said to have started into strong westerly winds which gave way to foggy conditions near America; it was a roasting hot day on the Sunday she docked. She covered the 3,300 miles in 14 days and 21 hours —an average speed of 9¼ knots. Not a very impressive speed. But New York was astonished that the new material and the new propulsion could do it at all.

The New York Herald was generous: a four-deck headline read: 'Arrival of the Monarch of the Ocean *Great Britain*. Brilliant Spectacle—Unparalleled Enthusiasm—Immense Concourse of Spectators.' Crowds were big, but might have been bigger if premature reports of the *Great Britain*'s arrival had not disappointed many. For those who turned out Captain Hosken provided a good view going up the North River, between the Battery and Governors Island. and then she was lost among the

masts on the East River. After waiting an hour for the ebb tide
to slacken, she tied up at a pier at the end of Clinton Street. As
a tribute to *pluribus in unum* each of her masts carried a different national flag—the Austrian, Russian, Spanish, French, as
well as the British flag on the mainmast and a Union Jack/Stars
and Stripes joint flag on the foremast. 'She is truly beautiful...
like a great castle above the water ... this most splendid vessel.'
The London *Times* man was jaundiced: 'I did not think she
looked very elegant with her six low masts. The graceful rig of
the American vessels is well known, and the *Great Britain* con-
trasted unfavourably in the opinion of many.'

The GWSSCo had an advertisement in Monday's paper for
paying customers to look over the ship. A committee of passengers headed by Colonel Everest, FRS, and including two US
Navy officers, presented a testimonial of their 'great satisfaction'
in completing a trip whose novelty 'gave rise to an excited state
of public opinion'. They noted particularly that the ship had
encountered headwinds and heavy seas for four days yet 'her
machinery never suffered the slightest interruption'. Captain
Hosken was given dinner at the Astor House and drank toasts
to, among other things, 'the pacific influence of steam—it makes
all nations neighbours and neighbours *should* never quarrel',
and 'the cities of Liverpool and New York—honorable competitors in commercial enterprise'. He left next day, 30 August
with 53 passengers for the return voyage which took a leisurely
15½ days.

One of the reasons why the return voyage was slow was because the main top mast was carried away from about half way
up during a gust of wind. Two of the crew were seriously hurt
trying to move the stump of the mast the next day, and one
man had his arm amputated for which he was compensated by
a £25 collection among the passengers. The *Illustrated London
News* reporting the incident said that owing to desertions of the
original crew just before the *Great Britain* left New York a
scratch company had been gathered and there were not enough
hands to cope. In addition Captain Hosken was understood to
be unhappy with the rig, which he intended to alter. 'The wire
rigging is not found to answer as well as had been anticipated.'
In a calm, said the I.L.N., 'she rolls tremendously'.

There was a fast turn-round in Liverpool and the ship was
outbound again for New York on 27 September. Again she

headed out in strong westerlies, and on 2 October her foremast was blown away. Towards the end of the voyage Captain Hosken found that he was in a strong northerly drift and in shallow water near Nantucket, and on 13 October took shelter not far from Martha's Vineyard. From there he took a pilot to reach New York where the ship arrived on the 15th.

On the 18th the *Great Britain* went into dry dock where her six-bladed propeller was found to be damaged. Did she damage it on the shoals near Nantucket, or was it too flimsy for the job? Whatever the cause two arms had come off close to the boss, and one of the 'palms' was missing from another arm. Nearly all the remaining rivets were loose. One palm was shifted over to the vacant arm opposite, to restore balance, and the *Great Britain* set out for Liverpool on 22 September with a spatchcock four-bladed propeller.

All went well for a couple of days with careful management when, at 11 p.m., 'we found something wrong with the propeller, and striking the stern post very hard; reversed the engines, and after two or three good thumps, the arms broke off ...' then, continuing from the log, on Friday 1 November, after making good progress under sail mainly, 'another of the arms of the propeller broke, leaving only one, I think the repaired one, and the arm of another with a small plate we had put on the end of it'. Mild rationing was imposed and it was estimated that 30 days' supplies existed without 'going on short allowance'. On 6 November the log records 'the propeller, or what is left of it, has done wonders, at times making four knots against a moderate easterly wind'; but that afternoon at 5.15 'the remaining arm of the propeller broke', leaving only the half arm and the small piece of another about two feet from the centre. The engines were stopped and the *Great Britain* sailed the rest of the way arriving at Liverpool after 20 days on 17 November. The passengers came forward with the customary testimonial—the ship's behaviour in rough weather was superior, and the food good. True, no doubt, but it was straining truth to claim, as the passengers did, 'that we are well pleased with the *Great Britain* in every respect'.

Brunel was not pleased. 'If she makes another bad voyage she is ruined,' he wrote. She went into dock to be modified in the light of experience. The most apparent change, and among the first to be finished, was to the sailing rig. Investing faith in the propeller, and knowing that the *Great Western* used her sails very little, Brunel regarded sail power as an auxiliary aid. Five of his six masts—called after days of the week starting with Monday—folded down to lessen resistance to head winds; only Tuesday was stepped to the keel, square rigged, and permanent. To compensate for any appearance of insecurity the rigging on all the masts was iron which it was claimed cut resistance in that department by two-thirds as compared with hemp. But the technique of making rope from wire was a long way from perfection—it resulted in rope that was of inconsistent quality and which was vulnerable to salt water corrosion.

There was another major attribute, described by Captain Claxton. 'Economy of labour is a principle which has in a great degree affected the mode of rigging both the *Great Western* and the *Great Britain*. Nothing is so difficult to handle under a variety of circumstances as the sails of a steamer, unless the engine be stopped, which can never be allowed in Atlantic steaming where onwards—and forever onwards—is the rule. The greater the number of masts the more handy the sails, the smaller the number of seamen required to handle them. If these ships had been rigged as ships ordinarily are the former (the *GW*) would require a crew of more than 100 seamen, and the latter (the *GB*) that of a large frigate. Divided as the canvas is, and reduced, the former only requires 20 seamen before the mast, while 30 are enough in the latter. In the *Great Britain* there is in fact but one sail, the square mainsail which under any circumstances can require all hands to furl it.'

These advantages did not sufficiently impress Captain Hosken, a mast and a half to the bad after two trips. He had the iron rigging replaced by hemp—wind resistance had been the least of his problems—and had masts Wednesday and Thursday replaced by a square rigged mast as big as Tuesday which was given a maintopmast and a topgallant mast with spars in place of the original single topmast. Instead of two square sails the *Great Britain* could now carry six. The three remaining masts carried the schooner-style sails—called spencers. These masts were no taller than before, but they lost their hinges and were, like the mainmasts, fixed at the keel; offsetting, or other arrangements must have been made so that the rear three masts avoided the propeller shaft. Although, as the *Manchester Guardian* said, 'her style of rig does not admit of nautical cognomen'; five masts were original design specification for the ship, 'some difficulty in adjusting' intervening. The *Great Britain*'s slow slide backwards towards a sailing ship had begun.

The remnant of the six-bladed propeller was taken off and the much heavier version of the same diameter—15 ft. 6 in.—with four blades put in its place looking much more in line with subsequent propeller practice. The engines—which had been conceded seldom developed over 600 horsepower of the 1,000 advertised—were altered to improve the steam pressure and make it easier to stoke the 24 fires (12 at the fore end of the boiler, 12 aft).

This was a major job. The GWSSCo thought it might hire Liverpool's chief exponent of iron ships, Mr John Grantham, to oversee the work; there was an immediate shriek from Brunel: 'I am afraid I must object more clearly than I before did to Grantham having anything to do with the alterations on the *Great Britain*. Field came down to me this morning to say that he had heard of Grantham's engagement and the possibility of his having anything to do with the work, and we both agreed that it would be dreadful. No power on earth will prevent its being generally reported in newspapers, and in all old women's gossip, in papers to the Institution of Civil Engineers, in every possible gossipy channel, that by the advice and opinion of Grantham such improvements were effected as to ensure the success of the *Great Britain* which was before a total failure— I know the man and his wanting and his weakness and the annoyance would be *insupportable*. Field was in a fever at the thought of it and couldn't stand it—we must send our own people, and I must beg that G......m is specially *excluded*. Guppy, if poor fellow he is getting to work, and the more work he has to do the better, must for his own sake take special care that nobody has anything to do with it. I will rather take it in hand myself—I will really without any joking or exaggerating. ... Pray think of Grantham and make me and Field easy.' Captain Claxton, to whom this letter was sent on 19 December 1845, makes several respectful mentions of Grantham's opinions in his own writing—maybe that explains Brunel's stridency.

Grantham was dropped, and Guppy went to Liverpool. He was sending gloomy news to Brunel by 20 April 1846 who, on the same day sent a dire warning to Captain Claxton: 'It seems from Guppy's letter that the boilers are not likely to be ready before the engines, and that it will be sharp work to get the engines ready for the 27th. Now if this is the state I must seriously and strongly urge upon the directors the propriety of at once making up their minds to postpone the day of sailing—however painful it may be, however annoying. No one will, I think, deny, that it would be much more injurious to the interests of the company to send the vessel again imperfect than to delay for a short time the first voyage this season—for in all probability it would only affect her first.

'No risk ought to be run. If she makes another bad voyage she is ruined in character and would remain on your hands unsaleable. I cannot myself conceive that there can be a doubt as to the necessity at any cost of delay in trying her, and in a hurry, but with certainty ascertaining her efficiency in every respect before she sails upon this voyage, upon the success of which depends little less than her whole value—probably as an even question of money £80,000 to £100,000 hangs upon the result. If you look at it in this simple light, the question of her sailing on the day advertised is not worth *consideration*, surely, in comparison with such a sum. And as regards feelings and credit, everything is in favour of delaying her day of sailing until we feel sure of her success. If we can get a trial day by the first, and if everything is right, she might either sail from the river without coming into dock, or come in on the 9th and sail on the 10th. But in the meantime you ought to write to America postponing the day. I trust the directors will do this. I am convinced it is *right*, and therefore may as well be done at once.'

This letter, too, was effective. Boards of directors usually did what Brunel told them. The *Great Britain* went into the Irish sea for a shake-down on 30 April proving the greater efficiency of the new propeller by steaming at 11⅜ knots with the great driving drum turning at 16¾ r.p.m. Coal consumption went down (it had been estimated at up to 80 tons a day for her first voyages) and there was more steam. In tests of speed the *Great Britain* beat the Cork steamer *Nimrod*, and the mail steamer *Prince* and kept up for half an hour with the reputedly fast iron steamer *Sea King*. She left for her third voyage to America on Monday 11 May with only 28 passengers on board and after four good days under steam one of the two engine air pumps broke. These cleared the condensers of air and water and maintained the vacuum to exhaust the cylinders without which low-pressure engines could not work. Proceeding chiefly under her better spread of sails speeds of over 11 knots were kept up. She docked on 29 May.

Turning around very quickly—considering the repairs to the engine—she left New York on 8 June with 42 passengers and made a fine passage back against headwinds in 13½ days under steam all the way; this was about the average length of passage of the *Great Western*. The passengers forecast future crossings in 10½ days in their testimonial, no doubt prompted by the captain. Going back again to America the ship was held up by fog but still got her 110 passengers over in 13½ days. There was a portentous mishap—she scraped a keel in the fog off the Newfoundland coast. There was trouble, as the season got under way, with the great spiked chains which geared up the engine r.p.m. by 2.95 to the shaft. In spite of Brunel's precise instructions about case hardening the joining pins and their sockets, being of iron the chains developed imperfections and stretched.

Chain-and-sprocket transmission was a compromise between the belt or rope drive that Brunel had hoped might do originally but which was not efficient for a power unit of 1,000 horsepower. Cogs in the *Archimedes* made such a din, and ran so roughly, that Brunel turned away from them. In keeping down noise and vibration aboard the *Great Britain* the chain drive succeeded. But when they got out of true the chains fractured the wooden teeth on the drums. Robert Stephenson pointed out to Guppy that they looked like big versions of drives he had used on some of his early locomotives 'which were discarded on account of their lengthening so much as to render them useless'. Brunel said that as a temporary expedient she could run on three instead of four chains.

An 18-hour stop to repair one of these chains was the only incident on the voyage back from New York which began on 1 August. In spite of this the *Great Britain* recorded the very good time of 13 days 8 hours.

It might just have been the beginning of modest commercial success. The ship went into dry dock to examine the effects of the Newfoundland scrape which were found to be nil and a certain amount of publicity was extracted from this for the safety of iron. This factor was shortly to be put to a supreme test.

CHAPTER III

Trouble in Ireland

Hitches had marred the first voyages of the *Great Britain*. But that was what first voyages were for. Nobody seemed to mind; her power as a sailing ship surpassed what had been expected and the *Great Britain* was able to overhaul other ships as impressively under sail as when her propeller was working. She was big, she was comfortable, and when she had completed four round trips potential customers evidently thought her safe. She set out on her fifth voyage from Liverpool at 11 a.m. on Thursday 22 September 1846 with exactly half her capacity of 360 passengers on board. This was the largest number she had so far carried and represented a record number for a steamship on the Atlantic run. The voyage ended in disaster as the *Great Britain* ran aground the Irish coast ten hours later. Three weeks afterwards Captain James Hosken, her commander, wrote to the directors of the GWSSCo: 'I take the whole blame, if there be any, to myself, for it is I alone who had anything to do with the navigation of the ship.'

It was a remarkable wreck. The only fatality was the Great Western Steamship Company. Otherwise not a soul was scratched. One man slept through the entire incident. It proved, in a way a decade of trouble-free trips could not, that iron ships were safer than wooden ones. And it provided the do-it-yourself and home-inventor brigade of early Victorian England with hours of harmless fun producing plans for getting her afloat again.

Those who experienced the grounding thought their end had come; ships hitting shores in those days were very much the equivalent of aircraft today hitting mountains. A girl passenger wrote from the safety of Liverpool on 26 September: 'We have indeed been in fearful peril. The newspapers by no means represent the extent of the danger. The ship struck the rocks at ten o'clock; I had just gone to my state-room, and the instant I felt the shock I knew something was the matter. In a moment there was a second shock, and all was confusion. Men and women rushed out, the latter from their berths, and some threw themselves into the arms of strangers. We could with difficulty stand. Mr ...'s first words to me were "I think there will be no loss of life, but the ship is gone". "I think there will be no loss of life!" What fearful words in a dark night, the rain falling, with wind! There was possibility, chance of it, then. Oh I cannot tell you of the anguish of that night! The sea broke over the ship; the waves struck her like thunderclaps; the gravel grated below. There was the throwing overboard of the coals, there were the cries of children, the groans of women, the blue lights, the signal guns, even the tears of men; and amidst all rose the voice of prayer—and this for long dark hours. Oh, what a fearful night! Thy mercy, Oh God, alone saved us from destruction. The day dawned and we lay between two long ledges of rock, while another stretched across our front. Five hundred yards to the right or left, two hundred yards in advance, and the ship had been dashed to pieces. Three hundred persons had perhaps been cast in that dense darkness amid the breakers. You cannot imagine such a scene. We cannot account for the accident, but the conduct of Captain Hosken through the night was admirable. The newspapers say that the ladies went to bed; some of them at the captain's urgent request, lay down in their dresses. Towards morning I did in my cloak upon the floor and covered with a blanket brought me by a passenger.

'At dawn we were lowered over the ship's side and carried on shore in carts of sea-weed manure. We walked through an Irish bog; and Mrs .... and I lay down upon the (wooden) floor of an Irish cabin where we found plenty of bread, some bacon, and an egg among three. At one time the Irish assembled in such numbers that we feared a riot. To my astonishment and gratitude all the luggage was saved.'

Another passenger said: 'The great majority of passengers were very ill; the Viennese children kept crying violently around Madame Weiss, and several passengers who ought to have shown firmness betrayed lamentable weakness. Captain Hosken continued cool and composed and several times referred to his charts. No one retired to rest—all were full of fears; but it was found next day that one passenger had never awoke till morning. At four o'clock in the morning boats came alongside and several persons went ashore; and as the tide receded men waded alongside and carried passengers ashore on their backs; several however wished to remain on board, but Captain Hosken insisted on their leaving the vessel as he could not be answerable for their lives.'

Captain Hosken must have been giving half a mind by this time to his own professional life. He had been in the Royal Navy and was for that reason a better employment prospect to bright new shipping companies who wanted nothing to do with scruffy masters of merchantmen. But Hosken had been in the merchant marine since 1831, first in command of a post office packet at Falmouth, then from 1832 to 1837 on foreign merchant ships. In 1837 he became captain of the *Great Western*. He had sheaves of complimentary letters from passengers, one from the GWSSCo, 'and a valuable present from the Underwriters at Lloyds for nautical skill and seamanship'. What went wrong?

And what, first of all, was he doing going to America from Liverpool around the north of Ireland when the route past Cape Clear and Baltimore was then, and later, more popular? 'I determined to go by the north channel,' he wrote, 'as the wind was certain to be south westerly in the south channel after passing Holyhead; and I have frequently taken the north channel before, and think it best under those circumstances; indeed I would take it in preference were all things equal. My reasons are in thick weather (and I have gone out of the north channel in fog) you meet one vessel in that channel to 20 in the south; indeed, with the first of a south-wester, one to 50. You cheat the tides, and have less against and more for you. You get clear of the land in much less time. You shorten the distance to New York a little, and you get a great advantage by being north, as the set of the Atlantic generally is to the Southward indeed almost invariably, and a slant of wind sometimes, as the wind hangs more to the northward than it does further south; on the whole it is my opinion that a day is saved in the passage by going through the north channel when the season for meeting field ice is over, and the ice bergs drift to the southward.'

The *Great Britain* got under way in a fine south-east breeze at the Mersey bar at ten past one. She sailed at a consistent 10¾-11 knots. The log was checked for accuracy. 'At about half past five,' Hosken reported, 'I caught a glimpse of the Isle of Man, but what part of the island exactly, or how far off, I could not decidedly say, as it was then getting dark, and the weather becoming thick. Immediately after, or about six o'clock, it came on to rain and blow harder, and the weather very thick, and it threatened to be, as it proved, as vile a night as could be experienced. I have no doubt this would be corroborated by anyone at sea on that night (the *Sea Nymph* would not start from Warren Point—a most unusual thing).

'About seven o'clock I remarked to the first and second officers (both of whom were with me on the forecastle, looking out, where I had been, and continued there and at the compass, with the exception of from five to ten minutes from half past five to the time the ship struck,) that we must be well up with the Calf, and that I might safely allow her 10½ knots since leaving the Bell buoy [where they dropped the Liverpool pilot]; soon after this I told the first officer to shorten sail at eight o'clock, take in top gallant sails, two reefs in foretop sail, one in the main, and haul the foresail up, as I should alter the course to N by E (which is higher than the north channel course) and go easy all night, feeling sure the ship was past the island. The course was altered at eight, and sail shortened accordingly; at about a quarter past eight I was standing by the wheel watching the steerage while reefing, when the officer looking out on the forecastle reported a light on the port, or larboard, bow; I said immediately it must be a vessel's light; the light was lost sight of in the thick weather for a short time and again shewed itself as a revolving light. I immediately kept the ship off her former course, NW by N, exclaiming "How is it possible she has not run her distance; what can have held her back?" taking the light for one of the Calf of Man lights, and supposing the other hidden by the thick weather, which is often the case as many seamen well know. I have been cruising on that station in a man-of-war some years since and frequently have seen but one light.

'I then continued by the compass watching the bearing of the light and trying with a glass to make out the second light, but a glass on that night was useless from the continued rain; I could not help thinking we must be past the island, at the same time there was a revolving light occasionally before my eyes to tell me *we were not past it*, and I did as I believe most sailors in my situation would have done (not knowing there was any other revolving light in the direction we had been running from the Bell Buoy, as my chart, new and dated 1846, does not shew any light on St John's point).

'I stood on until I got the right bearing for rounding the Hen and Chicken rocks laying off the Calf of Man. I then hauled the ship up to north gradually, and to N ½E ultimately when I was surprised to find on inquiring the time that it was a quarter past nine; I ran down for a moment to look at my chart, and back again to the helm, when I heard a loud hail from the forecastle, and at the same moment I saw what appeared and proved shoal water alongside. I instantly sung out hard a port—stop her; this was done. I ordered a back turn, braced the yards by, and shifted the helm, all without effect. The sea began to break over us and the engineer told me he could not move the engines; this made our case for the time hopeless as it was near high water on a spring tide. I then ordered the anchor to be got clear, the sky-lights, hatchways, companions, etc to be secured; the boats to be looked to, to be ready in case of need.

'I went below to assure the passengers that I believed there was no danger of loss of life provided they did as I wished them, namely remain quiet until daylight should shew us where we were and what was best to be done. I also consulted my own chart but could not make out to my own satisfaction clearly where we were, but believed we were not far from Ardglass, near Gun Island, and that the light in sight was that of the South Rock; and at daybreak when the Coast Guard people and others came off, I would not believe we were in Dundrum Bay, and that there was a light on St John's Point, for some time. The ship was forging ahead with the sea, and I was afraid to let the anchor go lest it might go through her bottom and do more harm than good—besides, the further the ship went the greater the chance there was of saving everybody. Towards daybreak it moderated and I immediately lowered one of our lifeboats and commenced landing the passengers, the ladies first. The tide soon ebbed out to the ship and the passengers got on shore in a variety of ways—by ropes, by carts, on men's shoulders etc.'

Reflecting on the cause of the accident Captain Hosken said that there must have been a 'westerly set'—drift—and that while the log showed only slightly less than 11 knots, the vessel had actually been making over 12. This meant that they did not see the Calf of Man lights at all. He absolves the compasses. His report said: 'I tried the compasses a day or two after we got here and found them correct to a quarter of a point.' The chief cause of the accident was the absence from his chart of the mark for a light on St John's Point.

A doubt was shortly afterwards cast on the validity of Captain Hosken's claim about this fatal omission. Mr J. P. Younghusband, a member of the Liverpool firm acting as underwriters for the GWSSCo, wrote: 'The channel chart in use on board the Great Britain at the time of her loss was 'published by John and Alexander Walker, Agents to the Admiralty, 72 Castle St, Liverpool and 9 Castle St, London, 1846', and Captain Hosken states in his report that the chart 'does not shew any light on St John's point'.

'On examining the channel chart now in the Underwriters' room here, which bears exactly the same title as mentioned above I find the light on St John's point is correctly and particularly laid down and as the directors in their minutes state that the omission of it was "the primary cause of the disaster" which befell the vessel I think it is due to all those personally interested that this point should be clearly ascertained, and I hope the chart used on board the *Great Britain* will be sent to Liverpool for the inspection of the underwriters upon her. The high character which the GWSSCo and Captain Hosken have hitherto enjoyed in the public esteem will make them very anxious that this discrepancy in the charts should be clearly proved.'

Mr Younghusband's point is not resolved in any records. The directors of the GWSSCo made a plea for public support for legislation to compel all who sold Admiralty charts to have them certified by inspectors that all known lights, buoys, and beacons were actually in place on the charts up to the time of the date stamp on them.

This was an outward-looking response by the GWSSCo to what they called 'the stranding of so noble a specimen of naval architecture'. It brought them face to face with the prospect of ruin—a prospect mitigated only by their having come close to facing it before. Their first reaction was pessimistic. In a letter to Hosken, Captain Claxton said that the board did not expect him to stay on board the ship 'in the state she now is', and that as 'soon as we hear from the underwriters that they agree with us to sell her as she stands' Hosken could leave. In the meantime 'all that is valuable copper and brass should be landed'.

There seemed a fair chance, however, that the *Great Britain* might be floated off and efforts were made to do this on the next spring tides—a week or so after she grounded—but a gale blew up and prevented the rescuing vessel—the *Sea Nymph*—getting near. It was then decided to get her further up the beach for safety and her sails were set. She was driven 'a considerable distance' in this way. Mr Alexander Bremner, a salvage expert, and Mr Paterson, the ship's builder, then put up breakwaters to protect the ship from the wind and water during the winter. Gales on the 19 November destroyed them. 'The directors upon this lost all hope of saving her and she was left' according to one recollection.

There was even a moment when the mercurial optimist Brunel doubted the usefulness of going to Dundrum. On 2 December 1846 he wrote to Claxton inquiring how to get to the vessel—'the process may not be so easy by land as it seems to be by sea. It is a great bore your not going. I am not sure that I shall because if it is all up my going can be no use or satisfaction to the company, and I question whether I ought to go merely for my own satis-faction.'

He did go to Ireland, however, and found that all was far from up. 'I was grieved,' he wrote to Captain Claxton, 'to see this fine ship lying unprotected, deserted, and abandoned by all those who ought to know her value, and ought to have protected her, instead of being humbugged by schemers, and under-writers.... The finest ship in the world, in excellent condition, such that £4,000 or £5,000 would repair all the damage done, has been left, and is lying, like a useless saucepan kicking about on the most exposed shore that you can imagine, with no more effort or skill applied to protect the property than the said sauce-pan would have received on the beach at Brighton. Does the ship belong to the company? For protection, if not for removal, is the company free to act without the underwriters? If we are in this position and we have ordinary luck from the storms in the next three weeks, I have little or no anxiety about the ship; but if the company is not free to act as they like in protecting her, and in preventing our property being thrown away by trusting to schemers, then please write off immediately to Hosken to stop his proceeding with my plans.

'As to the state of the ship, she is as straight and as sound as she ever was, as a whole.... I told you that Hosken's drawing was proof to my eye that the ship was not broken; the first glimpse of her satisfied me that all the part above her 5 or 6 feet waterline is as true as ever. It is beautiful to look at, and really how she can be talked of in the way she has been, even by you, I cannot understand. It is positively cruel; it would be like taking away the character of a young woman without any grounds whatever.

'The ship is perfect, except that at one part the bottom is much bruised, and knocked in holes in several places. But even within three feet of the damaged part there is no strain or injury whatever.... There is some slight damage to (the stern), not otherwise important than as pointing out the necessity for some precautions if she is to be saved. I say "if', for really when I saw a vessel still in perfect condition left to the tender mercies of an awfully exposed shore for weeks while a parcel of quacks are amusing you with schemes for getting her off, she in the meantime being left to go to pieces, I could hardly help feeling as if her own parents and guardians meant her to die there.... What are we doing? What are we wasting precious time about? The steed is being quietly stolen while we are discussing the relative merits of a Bramah or a Chubb's lock to be put on at some future time. It is really shocking.'

Perhaps one example will show sufficiently what he meant about being humbugged by schemers. John MacIntosh proposed to blow the ship into deep water with gunpowder. He wanted to build a semi-circle of boulders round her bows supporting 'concave vessels'. These would direct the water, when the explosion occurred, towards the ship. The expansive force of the detonation would, he said, 'heave up a mass of nearly 2,000 tons of water which will form an artificial wave rolling from the embankment upon which the ship is carried from her position and placed in deep water. Large masses of water are heaved up at intervals by the ignition of powder'—the *Great Britain*'s course to the sea being between banks of gunpowder set off as she went by to sustain the artificial wave. Steam tugs were to have the job of helping, with ropes astern, in getting her to a place of safety. Brunel had to have forms printed regretting that he could look at no schemes, because so many were addressed to him.

There were, said Brunel, two alternatives: the GWSSCo could either sell the ship at Dundrum and get only 'hundreds' for her, or remove her to a port and near facilities for restoring her in which case she might be worth up to £60,000. Brunel's estimate of the cost of putting the *Great Britain* right was £8,000. But, he wrote, 'the mode of getting the vessel off the shore and into port is quite secondary to the consideration of how to preserve it where it is so that it may be in a condition to be removed, and to be worth removing when the means of doing this are ready'. Which could not, he said, be less than three months.

So ... 'what I recommend is to form under the stern and along the exposed side of the vessel a *mass of faggots* made of strong and long sticks and used in the manner which has been so successfully practised in Holland against the sea. Eight to ten thousand faggots, 300 or 400 fathoms of 1-inch secondhand chain cable, 300 or 400 sharpened quarter-inch rods, and 4,000 bags filled with sand and the *Great Britain* would be as safe,' said Brunel, 'as if in a dock.'

Knowing that the *Great Britain* survived from her 90th year 35 years of Falkland Island storms without the protection of a single faggot makes Brunel's advice seem melodramatic. But his thinking was straight. 'You have a valuable piece of property lying on a most exposed shore. If preserved for a few months that property will in all probability be worth £40 or £50,000. If neglected for a few weeks longer it will probably be worth *nothing*. Can you as men of business under such circumstances waste your time at this moment in discussing what you will do in three months hence, and what plan you will then adopt to take your property to market but will you not rather first and *immediately* adopt decisive steps for *preserving* the property and then consider what you had best *do with it*.'

This broadside got the GWSSCo sitting upright again. It sanctioned the breakwater scheme and posted Captain Claxton to Dundrum to manage the work with the assistance of an almost daily exchange of letters with Brunel in which he addressed himself to the humblest details. 'I hope you are getting furze bushes in good quantities. Place the faggots always at right angles to the surface to face the sea with the sticks as you would an enemy with your bayonets.'

The ship was saved and thoughts turned to getting her off. Brunel—in spite of warning the owners against doing this—had himself considered what ought to be done. He concluded that the best approach would be 'to lift the vessel by mechanical means, to lay ways under her, and to haul her up sufficiently far to be safe from the sea, to repair her just sufficiently to make her watertight—then launch and bring her to Liverpool or

Bristol'. What is here outlined in a sentence took eleven months in all to achieve—months of thankless sweat against the attrition of the sea, months of irritation at the pace of life and some of the inhabitants of rural Ireland, the whole mix fermented to explosive consistency by a neurotic Scots salvage expert.

To marine experts in the 1840s, the protection and not the rescue of the ship was, as Brunel said it should be, the important matter. A Royal Navy and a Royal Engineers officer were separately sent to look at the breakwater and report. Conditioned by the vulnerability of wooden ships and noting the savagery of the storms that swept Dundrum Bay they did not hesitate to credit the breakwater with the saving of the *Great Britain*. Captain Claxton got to work organising the breakwater to protect the stern and starboard flank of the ship as soon as he arrived. He began piling up faggots (bundles of small sticks about 11 feet long and 20 inches in diameter) but could not keep them in place; one of the iron lifeboats from the *Great Britain* was used, filled with sand, as a weight, the great driving chains from the engine drums were used, but the faggots either sank or were washed away. Brunel's 'bayonet' scheme was ineffective too. Captain Claxton then developed the idea of using flexible young timber as a sort of cage behind which the faggots could be placed, and as an elastic breakwater absorbing the worst impact of the rollers. This 'cradle of green beech poles' was planted three thick at the most exposed places, then two thick, and then in a single row. Eighty poles were used (at 12s. apiece) and 5,800 faggots (at 6d. each and 6d. cartage).

Looking back the following April at the winter's work on the breakwater, Captain Caxton said present tasks were 'child's play compared to the work we went through in frost and snow and hail and storm—the thermometer at 25 when at work more in than out of the sea: but there was no flinching then neither will there be with such fellows until she floats or sinks; each man feels and acts as if success depended upon himself and it will be my fault if he loses the idea'. The job was well done because in June Captain Claxton wrote: 'We are in the act of removing all the breakwater except the outer tier of spars—such a sight was never seen—granite, solid granite would be easier to break away than the foundation. And over it by and by the ship has to be lifted!!!'

On the 17 June 1847 Captain Claxton wrote a report for the

Admiralty outlining the situation, the events that had led to it, and his plans for the future. 'Since the early part of April all our efforts have been directed to tightening her from within, the whole of her leaks being below the level of the sand and water, and in getting up portions of the machinery and otherwise lightening her by discharging sand and coals as the same could be got at on low tides as her head came up. The great object as regards expense being to ascertain exactly what power of lifting could be relied upon before deciding upon the amount of exterior application. By degrees, and after about one or two trials at the top of the springs since the end of April we have succeeded in raising her exactly 4 ft. 6 in. forward and in gradually relieving her of about 500 tons which when I commenced was beyond our reach, being always under water. About 50 tons of machinery have been landed at Liverpool, and about 40 tons more await a vessel hourly expected.

'The lightening process has progressed so far that the whole of the after part of the ship, the coal bunkers, the upper forehold, and the forward compartment of all may be considered completed, and on Monday last upon an ordinary spring she rose a full foot forward and she would have risen higher aft if it had not been prudent to let the water run there from the engine room so as to assist in lightening her forward where alone the bottom is damaged, and at the same time keep her at rest aft in her present position under the protection of the breakwater.... The great difficulty we have had to encounter has been to prevent her settling into her dock after floating; this has been overcome by heaving her hard over to the port against the side of her dock and when she was at the highest shooting about 30 tons of large stones previously placed on each occasion on slides or stages at low water and canted with entire success at where her angle is great into the space vacated by her rising. Immediately the tide sufficiently receded a vast number of stones were thrown and pushed under wherever there was a vacancy.

'I consulted with Mr Brunel and two plans were discussed; one to raise her on spars with purchases to crabs, each equal to lift about 15 tons, the other to apply solid timber from the sand to the 14 ft. mark and to fill her engine room and lower hold with cork.... By the 15 May she was gradually raised until she reached 44 in., 39 in. of which were maintained and the largest hole, that under the fore corner of the boilers (which have been

raised 14 in. by the rock that made it) was got at and effectually
stopped—the difference of the levels afterwards on a 13½ ft. tide
being 6 ft. in favour of the ship in the engine room without
pumping. Still there are other holes, and fearful of the responsibility, and of the season running away, I requested that Mr
Bremner might be sent to my aid. He was met at my request by
Mr Paterson, the company's ship builder. Mr Bremner brought
a plan expecting that he would have to raise about 2,000 tons;
finding however that three quarters of that had already been
accomplished that plan modified was discussed and eventually
with an improvement suggested by myself passed, if not quite
approved, by Mr Brunel.

'It consists of weighing her up by suspending a number of
large boxes to spars, a pair to a box, each box large enough to
hold about 40 tons of sand which by doubling the suspending
chain will have the effect of 80 tons less the friction as the ship
rises on a spring high. The boxes will descend as the tide leaves
and if she does not quite stand off the ground she will be so far
up as to enable us to pack under with stones, beech trees, or
spars, and if necessary to apply screws in aid. If we do not
succeed in suspending her sufficiently to patch from without.
there is scarcely a doubt of our succeeding in getting rid of all
the sand and getting at what holes there may be from within.
The improvement suggested upon this, which is in fact self
acting and simple in application, was to bevel the boxes to the
shape of the ship's bottom by putting a top to them when done
with as weights in the air they will avail themselves as camels
(floats) for floating her off when sufficiently tight. Twenty boxes
are made or making ... weighing each not much less than three
tons.'

And so Captain Claxton's report continues evenly in the
measured tones of a consul or a regional manager explaining
how some distant problem is being dealt with. This detachment
belies the man and his situation. He was weary of the set-backs
and disappointments—'I want rest and change ... I cannot quit
of course' was his comment on 29 May. His position was difficult,
as Brunel's chief executive in a rescue attempt being master-
minded entirely by post. Without being a salvage expert or
engineer he had to step in with practical answers to match
changing conditions although uncertain whether they would
counter Brunel's schemes, or work at all. He had the world's

biggest ship on his hands, but apart from a small core of English craftsmen, local skills—not to mention temperament—hardly met the case. 'We have such a set of carpenters to deal with; I do not know which are the worst, the men who come far, drink whiskey, sulk, and are insolent to poor Mr Bremner under whom they work, or the hedge-men we find hereabouts.'

It was as a deliverance from some at least of these pressures that Captain Claxton sought the help of the Bremners—James, the father, and Alexander, the son, from Wick, Scotland, men with 'more experience in raising and removing wooden built ships than probably any other.' But they only added to his troubles. First it was noted of Bremner senior, 'the fact is he sleeps on board to be always at his work to which he is a perpetual slave'. Then Captain Claxton confided to Brunel 'I wish we had stuck to heaving over and stoning up and lament much to see her pinned between the spars and boxes in which, seeing how they are slung, I begin to lose faith'. Finally, faced with a threatened walk out by the crew on Bremner's account—which he prevents—Captain Claxton says 'I have great trouble with heads of departments neither the Intendant General of Iron Works, the head of Woods and Forests, nor the chief of the Naval Department square with poor Mr Bremner who is indefatigable and expects everybody's heart to be as much in the business as his own ... they have all felt they were themselves entitled to more merit than they now feel is awarded to them.... Oh that it were ended.'

With this cauldron bubbling under him Captain Claxton, at the end of his report to the Admiralty, converts some of his anxieties into judgments about the lifting equipment. 'According to rule they should lift nearly 1,200 tons by doubling the suspending chains, they will not, however, do anything like that for the friction must be immense. On the other hand when attached to her bottom as camels they should float fully 500 tons which will raise her sufficiently to get her off on an ordinary spring tide; on a high spring tide of 15½ ft. she would, if tightened, be altogether afloat without outside application of any sort.' The month of June goes out with the comment that Bremner 'is much cut up and begins to find out that it is likely to be a far more serious job than he first expected'. They are behindhand with the box-work but wise to attempt no premature trial 'with gentlemen of the press daily visitors'.

July arrives and there are only two original crew members left and Captain Claxton fears the Bristol carpenters will strike or have to be sacked for 'insolence to Mr Bremner'. Bremner himself is reported 'almost worn out with anxiety ... his estimate (£460. os. 10d.) ... will be quadrupled and I see it wears him as much as the carpenters and the labourers annoy him'. The work went ahead somehow. Screw jacks were applied at the bow of the *Great Britain* working on her anchor holes. Amidships at low tide rows of levers stick out like oars from a Roman galley; these are fulcrumed on deep-sunk piles to purchase on the ship's bottom through heavy weights—a sand filled lifeboat on one side—placed on the lever ends. These levers produce technical problems for Claxton because as the tides come in the levers on the port side move 'six or seven feet' and 'I am obliged to keep her full, as if she moved or played much it would be fatal to the boxes and spars'. Brunel was not impressed: 'I do and have all along,' he wrote on 7 July, 'felt very anxious about old Bremner's proceedings. The *Great Britain* is bigger than anything he has had to deal with, and I fear that until he has positively *felt* the weight, his mind is not one capable of feeling by figures. All that you describe of his levers appears to me at this distance childish. Like driving in a tenpenny nail with spun yarn. I shall rely most upon you getting the vessel light.'

As Captain Claxton modestly put it the night before the major lift-off attempt, 'It is nervous, most nervous, work'. All was to be put to the test on July 12, and this is what happened: 'Our first effort with boxes and levers was made today. 9.10 a.m. She begins to move, the tide having risen to 11 ft. and with these soundings; now as it required 13 ft. before she rose on the last occasion, it is quite clear that the levers and screws have prized her. I write as events occur, tablets in hand. 9.50, Up forward 3 in., boxes beginning to drop, noise awful. 9.30, Up 5 in. 10 o'clock, Up one foot. 10.15, Up 1 ft. 4 in. 10.25, 1 ft. 8 in. 10.40, 2 ft., water 13½ ft. balks bending a good deal, feel certain the boxes will not come up if the ship falls too much with the tide. 10.45 still rising, a balk on the port side springing, advised with Mr Bremner and opened all valves, knocked out the shores of the large one to stop her rising. The water flew as high as the deck.

'11, all is now quiet. 11.20 it is now high water, the tide rose to 14½ ft., the three large screws have an immense pressure on them from the weight of the water let in since there were hove when she was up highest; can they stand it when she drops as she will, a foot or so, for we have nothing but stones to drop under her? The levers are dropped much, and they are down between three and four feet; if the ship settles a foot the boxes should come up two ft. or something must yield to that extent; it will be an awful trial, as the friction with such small sheaves [pulley wheels] will be enormous. Mr Bremner says each screw will hold 100 tons weight.

'11.40, Tide begins to fall, foremost starboard balk splits, box gone with a crash, grand, indescribable, after chain as before cut through outer planks. 11.50, Another balk gone, another crash, another box down. 11.55 ditto, ditto. 11.57, ditto, ditto. 12, Another, I fear they will all go for there has been no yielding back. I have chalked chains and balks and not one inch has one of them come up—they must be made lighter before we raise her higher or we shall have no camelling from them. 2 p.m. The ship went back a foot and so stands a foot higher. Five boxes altogether gone and seven balks; only one chain broke—the half link struck the rim of my hat—a link shot.'

Undeterred by basic limitations revealed in the first trial of his lifting system, Mr Bremner at once began adding to his gadgetry. Trenches were dug under the front of the ship, filled with stones, and topped off with hard wood platforms like a series of railway sleepers. On these were placed remotely controlled keel wedges. More piles were sunk, and the sides of the ship drilled for fixing points for what was called the self-acting shore. Its outer end would be drawn in automatically as the ship rose to provide a higher level of support. Eye bolts were put in the ship's bottom so that rope operated wedges could be pulled downwards to give support. Wooden chutes with remotely controlled ramming hammers were built to carry stones under the ship as she rose, making a sequence of stone cradles under the heaviest parts.

Captain Claxton's comment was that the chutes used up all the wood intended to seal off the sand-boxes as floats, and he questioned the usefulness of loading the ship with stones for sliding down the chutes when so much effort had been devoted to making her light. He did not obtrude these points and the augmented collection of pre-Heath Robinsonia was ready for the high tide on 29 July when she came up a planned 2½ ft. But, wrote Claxton, 'the tide this day would have done the work for us without anything, or nearly so, for she has never been so tight'.

Making the *Great Britain* watertight was the solution Captain Claxton had most faith in. He wrote of John Crew, the foreman boilermaker. 'Nothing can be conceived more trying than the way he has been obliged to manage. His head, and the head of his helpers, on one side, down close to the water, the sides of their faces sometimes in it, as they lay on their sides they can each use only one arm and with that they grope for holes or slits under water and through the sand, judge the dimensions, prepare a plate for the next tide with a long bolt in the middle with nuts and screws slip it through, then heave it up. Of course the failures are frequent and the draw upon the health greatly for the stuff at the bottom is most foul. But he perseveres and in most cases his determination and indomitable courage is repaid by success. I do not permit the Bremners in the slightest degree to interfere with him, or trouble him.'

In all, the lifting efforts raised the *Great Britain* 8 ft. 7 in. credit for which Captain Claxton distributed to Brunel for 4 ft. 6 in. and to the Bremners' contrivance 4 ft. 1 in. Having at last got a sight of the large holes under the engine room he decided to abandon efforts to mend it and to rely instead on making the inner skin of the double bottom watertight at a cost he notes of '100 tons more to carry'. Shortly afterwards Captain Claxton decided to abandon the idea of using the sand-boxes for floats— only four of the 20 could be made watertight and these four only half performed what was expected of them. In their place he looked for ships that could be lashed to the *Great Britain* to give her buoyancy, and after looking at five, acquired the *Margaret*, and the *John and Isaac*.

By this time—mid-August—the Navy had arrived in response to Captain Claxton's asking for two powerful steamers with hawsers for towing and a small tug for steering. Eighty-seven dockyard workers from Portsmouth, 25 of them from HMS *Victory*, left the steamer *Birkenhead* in the paddle box boat under Assistant Master Attendant Bellamy from Portsmouth. Captain Claxton was among his own and praised the sailors work. They brought a great many pumps (23 two-man, six four-man and two two-man) but on the night of the first serious effort to float the *Great Britain* off—abandoned at midnight on 25 August—the leaks beat the pumps. An attempt the next day moved the ship 'exactly five feet'. The supporting vessels kept breaking free, but this was no problem compared with the discovery that the *Great Britain* was still trapped in a rock basin. Men were employed to dig a gulley from the vessel's stern out to deep water. Captain Claxton found that just under the ship's stern the channel got no deeper in spite of the many men working—investigation showed it to be 'solid rock which prevented her moving more than five ft. on the last trial ... which the Irish looked to as a certain means of preventing the repeal of a union by which they had so greatly profited'. Profited to the extent of 1s. 3d. 'per tide' for labouring, and being allowed, the poorer among them, to take away the breakwater wood for nothing.

Although appalled by discovering a bar of rock at this crucial point in the operation lying directly in the path of the *Great Britain*, Captain Claxton felt fairly sure it could be removed with explosives. Worse was to come. After the trial ended James Bremner asked for an interview and delivered formally the verdict—shared by his son—that it would be 'hopeless to proceed further'. They felt that she would overleak her pumps and Mr Bremner said that this was the opinion, too, of the repair crew. No amount of optimism from Claxton would make the salvage expert alter his fixed notion. Captain Claxton immediately—this was three in the morning—went to the ship's engine room and found that when the ship moved off the props and stones and other supports she had opened out a half inch from the fore bulkhead; through the resulting slit much of the original packing had been forced by water pressure. 'Mr Crew and the whole of the men went to work and it was all finished before the tide came up.'

This last hurdle as quickly cleared as it had suddenly appeared, Captain Claxton was able to write on 27 August, 'Huzza, huzza—you know what that means'. With the help of 20 coastguard men manning the pumps the *Great Britain* had floated out on a 15 ft. 8 in. tide. 'She rose easily, therefore, over the rock ... but ... was clear of it by only five inches which shows how near a squeak we had.' Most of the crews of the two warships *Birkenhead* and *Scourge*, sent to help, were on board the *Great Britain* pulling ropes fixed to anchors. The *Birkenhead* was backed up to give a tow, and all the boxes and balks were taken down. The order 'heave' was followed by 'heave with all your might', and three cheers came after the announcement

'She's all your own my boys'. There was a momentary panic when they thought she had gone aground again—but the check came from the anchor Captain Claxton threw out. He wanted her beached for a final examination of her bottom. 'Tomorrow,' he wrote, 'shall see her free!! And Mr Bremner's fears either corroborated, or, as I hope, proved false alarms—he is very low, but I shall cheer him up by and by.'

On the Friday evening it was planned to test the pumps at the *Great Britain*'s new berthing place, 170 yards seaward of the scene of the long struggles with her. All the supporting vessels, boxes, rafts, and casks, assembled to lift her were put aside. Because of a row about wages only 36 instead of the 120 Irish expected turned out 'under their long tried foreman James McGenis' to man the pumps. Sailors volunteered to take their places and got paid their wages. The tide rose quickly and when he heard that seven pumps were holding their own, Captain Claxton decided to take her out into deep water. He put up the agreed light signal to fetch more RN men who duly arrived. She was hauled out, and her sails were set; voyage five was under way again eleven months behind the timetable.

It might have ended just as disastrously. The sailors had to leave the pumps to handle the ship and a dispute started among the pumping hands which did not end when two of the ring-leaders were forced over the side into the coastguard boat. At 2 a.m. Captain Claxton found that he had been 'at the mercy of the leaks for three full hours, for the pumping of the Irish was next to useless they all the time discussing where they were to be taken to, and how much to be paid. Consequently when the ship was taken in tow at 4 a.m. there was six feet of water in the engine room, and the ship for some time went on making at 4 in. per quarter of an hour.' More men were put to the pumps—enough 'to postpone the swimming point by a day and a half'.

In spite of the four-fold improvement obtained at the pumps, Captain Caffin of the *Scourge* recommended grounding the *Great Britain*. Captain Claxton turned her head for Liverpool, but soon after had to acknowledge that the numbers of men on board were not enough to keep the pumps manned in relays for a trip across the Irish sea. He decided instead to make for Strangford Lough, the entrance to which came in sight at 7 a.m.

It vanished from view almost at once when the densest fog Captain Claxton ever experienced came down and blotted out not only the land but the *Great Britain* from the *Birkenhead*. This led to a further change of mind, and the little convoy decided to head for Belfast with the water gaining fast in the *Great Britain*'s engine room. Twice on the way the two vessels sheered sideways together about a mile—the *Great Britain* was steering with a rudimentary rudder made from planks nailed to her main yard fixed at her stern. If this sort of drift had set in during the passage through the narrow entrance to the Lough, the results would have been serious. Captain Claxton said that the fog was 'a timely deliverance' from that hazard.

Arriving in Belfast without further incident, the *Great Britain* was put down safely on the mud. Two hundred men were hired and by 2 a.m. on the Sunday morning, 29 August, she was pumped dry. At 11 a.m. the same day she was on her way to Liverpool with a crew of 300, including a large number of those hired to pump out. The crossing was made at 6½ knots and there were no incidents until the Mersey was in sight; then the wind freshened and a couple of cables to the *Birkenhead* snapped and there was alarm in case the *Great Britain* broke free until the Liverpool pilot boat lashed herself to the stern of the rescued giant to act as a more effective rudder. She was then towed down to Prince's Dock and allowed to sink on to a grid iron. The squalls that began as she came down the Mersey developed into gales that went on for two weeks.

Although its great ship had been recovered at last, the GWSSCo was finished. The *Great Western* made only two voyages to America after the grounding of her consort. She was sold to the West India Royal Mail Steam Packet Co in April 1847 for £24,750—having cost £53,000 nine years earlier. Surveyors said it would cost over £21,000 to put the *Great Britain* back into commission, adding that no wooden ship could have survived such a stranding—they found six main holes varying in size from 2 ft. x 1 ft. to 5 ft. 9 in. x 1 ft. 4 in., plus other 'formidable' ones. They, too, praised John Crew's 'extraordinary performance', exhibiting 'the greatest ingenuity and perseverence'. And they said her iron structure 'must have been of the most excellent quality'.

The Irish won no praise during the Dundrum incident. The Admiralty received a message from one of the many naval officers detailed to help in the recovery 'that no confidence can be placed in the Irish who thwart all efforts for saving the *Great*

Britain in order to keep her at Dundrum for their own benefit'. In their defence it should be said that Ireland was enduring at that time the worst of the famine, the most devastating event in that country's sad history. The need of the Irish for the benefit of 1s. 3d. per tide for sand shovelling was acute. And they did get one creditable mention after the first reports of the grounding came in 1846 in the form of a newspaper correction: 'We take this opportunity,' it read, 'of contradicting upon the authority of an eye-witness the statement which has appeared in most of the accounts—that the peasantry behaved like savages. This is far from the fact; they did scramble for the luggage in the same way that London cabmen would if not kept in order by the police. In the above case passengers had the annoyance of seeing their baggage separated and carried off in all directions; but although this was very trying to witness, and occasioned damage in some instance, still it was done with a view to *saving* the property, and no stealing or wrecking took place.'

And when it came to awareness of the rate for the job, the Irish were guilty only of thinking more quickly than the English. On 5 November 1847 Mr Bellamy of the Portsmouth Dockyard sent the Admiralty a letter he had had from the GWSSCo 'reporting that £107 had been placed to his credit for distribution amongst the riggers employed in extricating the *Great Britain*, and complains of the inadequacy of the reward for their services'. The Admiralty thought the men should be satisfied. Mr Bellamy then asked to be relieved of the responsibility for dividing the money. The GWSSCo directors considered how it should be shared out, told the Admiralty, which ordered Mr Bellamy to comply.

Captain Claxton had worked himself out of a job when the *Great Britain* sank on to the grid in Prince's Dock. Apart from his good sense, loyalty, patience, and tact in applying Brunel's instructions at Dundrum, there was a deeper link between the two men. When the *Great Western* was undergoing final trials in 1838 fire broke out in the engine room. Brunel started to climb down to see what was wrong and fell 18 ft. ... on top of Claxton, whose body prevented what might easily have been a fatal fall. On 3 December 1847 Brunel wrote to Claxton saying, 'I enclose a long and rather full list of "instructions", I shall be glad to hear from you frequently'. Eight years later there was a more precise hint of Claxton's position when Brunel wrote, 'I should offer you £250 a year and your actual expenses for your time and services rendered to me in all matters connected with steam navigation, or nautical and ship matters'.

As for the Bremners, they had recovered sufficiently from their belief that the *Great Britain* would never float again to be proposing, in September 1847, to write the definitive account of their great success. It was partly to foil this ambition that the GWSSCo brought out an account of the rescue, in the form of an abridgment of the Brunel-Claxton correspondence. Brunel commented: 'I should not think the Bremners were book-writing men; though they may be penny-a-liners'.

The verdict of the *Nautical Magazine* was severe—and correct —'had her commander ... stopped his vessel's way as a seaman would have done, and found out what light it really was, feeling his way cautiously with his lead, the *Great Britain* would not have run headlong on to the strand. The absence of a light from a chart seen plainly and distinctly before a vessel would never occasion her loss in the hands of a careful commander in moderate weather when she is under the control of sail and rudder. But the *Great Britain* seems to have darted from her port anxious to run her course like a high-mettled racer.'

As with aircraft today, the easiest answer is 'pilot error' when doubt about cause of an accident arises. Nobody had died at Dundrum so there was no need for an inquiry. Doubts continued to trouble maritime authorities about the exact effects of iron ships on compasses. But no accident at sea was traced unmistakably to an error in the compasses caused by iron, so nothing was done—until the new iron ship *Tayleur*, 234 ft. long by 39 ft. broad, and bound for Australia hit the Irish coast in January 1854 with the loss of 290 lives among the 528 on board. She had set out on the nineteenth, got caught in a southerly gale, gone to and fro between the Isle of Man and the Skerries on the Irish coast to ride out the storm. Coming out of thick weather the *Tayleur* was unable to get away from the shore. She dropped both anchors, but the chains gave way, and she was driven on to the rocks.

The cause of the disaster was reported by the subsequent inquiry to have been 'the master making his calculations and placing his position on the chart upon the supposition that the compass before the helmsmen was correct. He was aware of the difference of two points between the compasses (there was another on the poop) but he knew not which was in error.' There was the usual rider that all would have been well if the lead had been used, and surprise that the owner did not have the ship swung after the cargo was put in.

John Gray (not the *Great Britain*'s captain), the most eminent Liverpool compass maker and fitter, told the inquiry that the original error on the *Tayleur*'s compass had been bigger than he had seen for a long time, 60° off the magnetic meridian. This, he said, 'was much larger than the *Great Britain* which was about 40 degrees'. Mr Gray had applied counter attractions to correct the compasses. But all he could say about the principles behind his corrections was that they were the same as he had used on 400 other ships—and that he had a certificate from Captain Mathews of the *Great Britain* speaking of her compasses in the highest terms.

Unsolicited testimonials would no longer do. The Liverpool Compass Committee set itself up at the end of 1854. Thomas Brocklebank was the chairman and there were 49 members including William Inman from the Shipowner's Association, representatives from the Literary and Philosophical Society, the Polytechnic Society, the Underwriters Association, and the Steam Ship Association. The committee was not certain what it was aiming at, but it gave three reasons for its coming into existence.

These were: 1. Methods of correcting compasses, especially for ships going to the southern hemisphere were unsatisfactory. 2. There were lots of sudden changes in compass bearings that needed looking into; and 3. It would be desirable to have full and trustworthy information about the effects on compasses of iron ships. The committee did not want to ruffle any experienced feathers so its first letter said: 'The committee feel bound to record as early as possible their conviction that the talents and energy of the captains of iron craft have generally been sufficient to overcome all difficulties arising from the magnetism of their ships, and to make the navigation of these vessels upon the whole as safe, if not so easy, as that of a wooden ship.

'It must not, however, be concealed that these difficulties have often been very great, and that the navigation of an iron ship on her first voyage particularly if it extend very far to the south severely taxes the care and prudence of her commander. At present it is quite uncertain until trial be made to what kind of compass errors a ship will be liable—whether they will be increased or diminished, or alter their character by change of geographical position; but from a variety of causes it is found that at present the experience of the captain of one ship ... is seldom or never applicable to the wants of another.'

As a start the committee gave forms to the captains of all iron and most wooden ships using Liverpool on which to mark compass deviations. A lot of iron was used in wooden vessels but it was 'extremely seldom' that anybody considered its effect though this had been known to exceed two degrees. It was equally unusual to swing a ship even when 600 to 1,000 tons of iron had been loaded, even though compass errors of up to seven degrees occurred in the compass before loading started. The Rev Dr W. Scoresby, FRS, was to do field work for the committee on a voyage in the *Royal Charter*.

Early optimism was replaced by sadder news in the committee's second report in 1856. It had encountered 'the apathy of shipowners, and the inertia or active opposition of persons interested in maintaining things as they are'. The forms so hopefully handed round met with a response from a comparatively small number of captains. But many of the difficulties in getting accurate information were overcome by painting compass bearings on the dock sides facing the river. These went from 180 degrees at Huskisson dock (then the most northerly) to 20 degrees at the inlet to Queens dock. These large figures were the bearings to Vauxhall Chimney in Everton, a chemical works demolished about 1910. They enabled the committee, and captains, to check compass errors. It was a facility that was widely and quickly mis-used, and a letter had to go out telling captains not to use the bearings to adjust faulty compasses— 'a complicated matter', it was pointed out.

Some progress had been made. There was now no doubt, the committee said, about the connection between a ship's magnetic characteristics and her position upon the building slipway. 'In all ships which have been examined, the north end of the compass invariably points towards that part of the ship which was furthest from the north while she was building.' It proposed to go on to discover how permanent those magnetic characteristics were, and what was the best position for building ships. In dealing with the permanence of the characteristics the committee immediately examined the *Great Britain*. It offered, 'the most striking case that can be quoted. This extraordinary ship had been stranded, strained, and altered; has traversed both hemispheres and been very many years in active service—yet her lines of no deviation are very much what Dr Scoresby would indicate them to have been while she was on the stocks.'

During the *Great Britain*'s major refit that ran into the winter of 1856-7, the owners, Gibbs, Bright, allowed the committee letting to take the vessel out of the Sandon graving dock, turn her round and put her back in. She underwent 'hammering in almost every part'. 'Yet how small is the change! A proof, apparently, that no circumstances can permanently conceal or greatly alter the direction of an iron ship's magnetism.' Quite a lot hung on this experiment, because in thanking Gibbs, Bright for the use of 'this noble ship', the committee said it was a chance long awaited—'it was thought by some persons that the lines of no deviation obtained in the graving dock were very much due to the ship's position at the time of the experiment and that by turning the ship end for end a considerable change in their direction would be exhibited. This is not in accordance with trials made in the same dock ... it has very little support from the *Great Britain*.'

When all the results had been evaluated the committee issued its third and last report (1857-60) which came to four conclusions: 1. Iron ship magnetism is distributed according to precise and well defined laws. 2. A definite magnetic character is imposed on every ship in building and never entirely lost. 3. Original magnetism is constantly subjected to small changes. 4. Compass errors can be compensated for successfully.

Poor and worn compasses caused as much trouble, however, as all other causes of deviation. The committee did away with 'the attraction of the land', 'compass disturbance from fog', 'unusual aberration', 'indraught', and 'other unfounded or imaginary pretexts which are now put forward when an iron ship gets stranded'.

Captain Hosken, banished to be harbour master, postmaster, and chief magistrate in the tiny newly-acquired island of Labuan, near Borneo, could take a little comfort from being perhaps the first cause of such important findings. He was by then, 1860, retired after having commanded a hospital ship in the Crimean War. It was appropriate that his indestructible ship should make such a significant contribution to the work.

CHAPTER IV

Steam Pioneers

British shipping was in a disreputable state when the Great Western Steam-Ship Company was founded in the spring of 1836. It was still recovering from the Napoleonic wars; but expectations of a genuine recovery were growing slighter as the total tonnage of the mercantile marine stayed obstinately within ten per cent of where it had been in 1815. Bigger ships had begun to appear, but foreign trade was very largely carried by vessels of between 400 and 500 gross tons; and these vessels not far removed in size and style from the *Mayflower*, were capable on a bad trip of equalling her 66 day crossing of the Atlantic.

American companies had set up sailing liner services that managed to reach New York from Liverpool in 36 days on average, and to make the eastbound crossing in 24 days. This kind of smart performance made little impression on British owners hiding complacently behind the heavily protective Navigation Laws; it made no impact at all on the scruffy and sometimes illiterate masters of British vessels who navigated by the seat of their pants and held despotic sway over crews of ragged and fatalistic simpletons.

One cause of the bad state of the industry was that it still lived in thrall of the eighteenth century when monopolies like the East India Company (Indian monopoly cancelled 1814) held exclusive trading rights executed in big armoured ships that made no concessions to commercial economy. The Falmouth Post Office Packet Service, which carried the mails over the Atlantic and such passengers as wanted to go, was a model of corruption. An inquiry in 1787 discovered that the Secretary to the Post Office had shares in the Packet Company and had collected £50,000; captains drew pay without going to sea, and crews supplemented wages with smuggling. During the French wars a new swindle—deliberate loss of ships for the insurance—was in vogue. By the mid-1830s the Admiralty was poised to take over the carriage of mails.

But it was American enterprise more than anything else that ensured Britain's failure to recover from the wars—in which she lost almost 6,000 ships. The Napoleonic wars provided the opportunity, and American foreign-going tonnage increased eightfold between 1789 and 1810. In building new, the Americans built their ships faster, though of less durable softwood; they could take products from India east across the Pacific to America, tranship them in New York, and sell them sooner and cheaper in London than the East India company. It was not allowed—but done all the same—because the British Navigation Laws forbade any but British ships from trading into British-held ports. These laws, abolished in 1849, contributed to the complacent state of British shipping.

As their ships became faster and bigger—they grew in the 25 years from 1815 from 500 tons to 1,200 tons register—the Americans devised new ways of operating them. They began to sail ships to a timetable. British ships still sailed when filled, when the wind was right, and when the captain came out of the inn. And the Americans ran ships to carry passengers. Leading this revolution was the Black Ball Line (founded 1816), with a scheduled sailing from New York for Liverpool on the first of the month. The Swallow Tail, Red Star, and Black X lines followed the Black Ball and by 1835 American ships were taking 50,000 emigrants a year from Europe, many from Liverpool, without a flicker of competition.

This was the background against which the GWSSCo issued its prospectus in January 1836, where its aim was announced as the setting up of 'regular lines of steamships between Bristol and those Western ports to which her geographical position renders her most eligible, the first to be directed towards the United States of America'. No detailed survey of the maritime situation, or weighing of factors survives from the beginnings of the company—the whole edifice, with its incalculable consequences, rests on a one-sentence riposte by Isambard Kingdom Brunel. At a meeting of the directors of the Great Western Railway Company in October 1835 someone remarked on the enormous length of the proposed London-Bristol line, at which Brunel said: 'Why do they not make it longer and have a steam boat to go from Bristol to New York and call it the Great Western?' This suggestion, says one report, 'was treated as a joke by most of those who heard it'.

It was a joke that is almost certain to have had roots in earlier discussions among the technically inclined GWR board members—Brunel himself had been pondering on steam ships for the previous six years. Within six months of Brunel's quip the board of the GWSSCo met for the first time.

From the outset the new company had difficulties to face which put a brake on the willingness of investors to put their money behind the promoters' enthusiastic predictions.

These difficulties were created by the Rev Dr Dionysius Lardner, a 44-year-old lawyer turned scientist from Dublin who had been for ten years professor of natural philosophy and astronomy at the newly founded London University. In 1840 he eloped with a Mrs Heaviside and was successfully sued by her cavalry officer husband for £8,000; and Thackeray satirised him as Charles J. Yellowplush, and as Dionysius Diddler. These claims to fame still lay in the future when he got in the hair of the GWSSCo by telling a December 1835 meeting in Liverpool that steaming across the Atlantic was impossible. The *Liverpool Albion* report said:

'The voyage from New York to Liverpool was, he had no hesitation in saying, perfectly chimerical and they might as well talk of making a voyage from New York or Liverpool to the moon. The vessels which would ultimately be found the best adapted for the voyage between this country and the United States would be those of 800 tons which would carry machines of 200 horsepower and would be able to stow 400 tons of coal. To supply a ten horse power (engine) daily required an expenditure of a ton of coals, and consequently 200 horse power would require 20 tons of coal daily; but if the vessel carried 400 tons of coal only it would not be practicable to undertake the voyage which would require the whole of the quantity. They must make an allowance of 100 tons for contingencies. Thus in reckoning the average length of the voyage which might be undertaken by such a vessel we might safely calculate upon 300 tons of coal which would be sufficient for 15 days and it might fairly be concluded that any project which calculated upon making longer voyages than 15 days without taking in a fresh supply of coals in the present state of the steamboat must be considered chimerical.'

Lardner pursued this theme at one of the early annual meetings of the British Association for the Advancement of Science held—as luck would have it—in Bristol in 1836. The local papers called the seven-day congregation 'the Wise Week'. This time he was a little less absolute in his use of language. He made deductions from figures obtained on the use of coal in the Falmouth-to-Corfu mail packets, considered the problem of using salt water in boilers and came to the conclusion that the utmost caution would be needed in steaming over to America and that '2,080 miles is the longest run a steamer could encounter—at the end of that distance she would require a relay of coals'. Brunel went to the British Association meetings and countered the propositions.

Whoever emerged from the exchanges as victor in the eyes of the assembled scientists, the consequences were bad for the GWSSCo. A note among the Brunel papers says: 'Unfortunately the prophecies of failure so confidently advanced by Dr Lardner not only expose the friends of the steamship to the harmless ridicule of his disciples, but also have a most prejudicial effect upon the subscriptions to the share capital of the company, and the original project of a line of steam vessels similar to the *Great Western* had to be abandoned for want of sufficient funds.' The original share capital of £250,000 was raised, however, and years later Captain Claxton wrote: 'The *Great Western*, in contempt of the elaborate and confident assertions of philosophers, at the meeting of the British Association in 1836 at Bristol, that it would be impossible for her to succeed in crossing the Atlantic, performed her voyage with the greatest ease to New York and back.' Samuel Hall, whose invention of a fresh water condenser for steamships—an important step forward—Lardner had also disparaged, was less oblique than Claxton. He got up at the 1837 BA meeting and called the Rev Doctor 'an ignorant and impudent empiric'.

Before dismissing Lardner as a nincompoop it is worthwhile recalling that Brunel's father, basing his judgment on a more respectable body of ignorance, thought the transatlantic steamer impossible.

Boats without sails can be traced back to the Romans. Records exist outlining Roman troopships moved by ox-propelled paddles; the Chinese had warships with man driven paddles. Leonardo da Vinci, inevitably, made drawings for paddle-wheel propulsion and—though he did not link the two—he made calculations for the expansive power of steam.

In the seventeenth and early eighteenth century references abound of schemes for boat propulsion by 'certain wheels on the outside' and devices 'profitable' when 'winds fayle'. A number of inventors thought of a windmill as a source of energy for turning a ship's paddles. John Allan in 1722 proposed water-jet propulsion. These all failed because the mechanical means of bringing them about did not exist. It was not until Newcomen and Savery pioneered the colliery pumping engine (first used in Dudley in 1712) and Boulton and Watt refined it after 1776 that the more delicate and complex application of steam afloat stood a chance of success. The extension of Watt's patent for 23 years to 1800 seems to have inhibited marine steam engine development in Britain.

For the Americans the steamboat became from the outset a means of fast internal transport. Development was rapid and by the 1840s it is thought that there was a greater tonnage of shipping on American rivers than was registered in the whole British Empire. These ships were powerful, to counter the currents, and had very shallow draughts—they would sail up valleys, it was claimed, 'only moistened by the morning dew'. These riverboats accentuated even further the slim clipper lines with a length to breadth ratio of eight or ten to one and gave vessels a fine entrance and a clear run to replace bluff bows and full sterns. Almost from Fulton's time speeds rose from nine to 13 m.p.h. There was an inevitable price to be paid for driving these ships hard on their primitive boilers—between 1816 and 1848 233 steamboats blew up on the Mississippi killing 2,563— the worst case was the *Louisiana* which exploded its boiler in New Orleans killing nearly 200.

This churning of paddles and sounding of sirens from 1815 was intense but very domestic. There were a few big steamers but by 1837 there were only 668 steamships in the United Kingdom with an average tonnage of 120. The weight of their machinery and their appetite for coal put limits on their usefulness. More than a dozen transatlantic voyages had been completed by the late 1830s by ships with steam engines. The *Savannah* (110 ft. long 320 gross tons) was the first across in 1819 to see if anybody in Europe would buy her (there was a trade depression in America). She set out on 24 May and on 18 June her log book states 'No cole to git up steam'. She took 27 days to reach Liverpool of which only 85 hours was under steam.

By this time steamships had become a nuisance and a Swansea meeting in December 1826 petitioned Parliament to protect sailing ships from 'further increase of steamers'. Steamers began to grow larger on the builder's slipways. The first Leviathan ship was the *United Kingdom* built as a London-Edinburgh packet. She was 160 ft. long with 200 horsepower engines by David Napier and she was the first steamer which attracted visitors to her building yard to marvel at her size. By 1833 the *Monarch* was being built for the General Steam Navigation Company's Edinburgh service and she was 206 ft. long—within two feet of the biggest ship in the Royal Navy.

Growth in the size of ships made iron a material for shipbuilders to consider because a strong iron ship weighed half as much as the same ship built of wood. Iron's beginnings were forced not by considerations of relative lightness and strength, but because timber was getting scarcer and dearer and iron cheaper and more plentiful. The *Aaron Manby* (116 tons burden, 120 ft. long) was built in Staffordshire in 1822, assembled in London and exported to France to work on the Seine as the world's first iron steamboat. In 1824 the Shannon Steam Packet Company was ordering iron ships and John Laird in Birkenhead founded his immense yard building iron ships; he built the *Garry Owen* (1834) for the Limerick-Kilrush run. It survived storm batterings and groundings that would have smashed any wooden vessel and helped the beginnings of a body of evidence in support of the superiority of iron. Iron ships were seen in remote regions—for exploring the Niger and Euphrates rivers.

More relevant to those who clearly saw what a money-spinner an effective line of steamships to America could be was the west-to-east crossing from Nova Scotia of the *Royal William*, also seeking a buyer. The voyage, in 1833, was made entirely under steam power and took 18 days. This was creditable, though not as fast as a good sailing clipper might manage on the west–east run. But her boilers had to be de-scaled of brine deposits every four days, an operation that took a whole day. This and other more southerly steam crossings of the Atlantic were freakish; the steamship had found its level as a ferry and a piece of port equipment for towing, disentangling, and berthing big ships. Dr Lardner's estimate of the chances of a transatlantic steamer must have seemed to many thoughtful listeners a fair statement supported by common experience.

Brunel tackled Lardner in the terms of the examples he had used about the Corfu ferry, pointing out how old they were and saying that speeds of $7\frac{1}{4}$ miles an hour could now be improved on by perhaps a quarter as much again. But this was unimportant detail. In recommending the building of a transatlantic steamer Brunel was arguing that 'the proportional consumption of fuel decreases as the dimensions and power of the engines are increased; consequently a large engine can be worked more economically than a small one. The resistance of vessels on the water does not increase in direct proportion to their tonnage. This is easily explained—the tonnage increases as the cube of their dimension, while the resistance increases about as their squares. So that a vessel of double the tonnage of another capable of continuing on an engine of twice the power does not really double the resistance—speed therefore will be greater with a large vessel or the proportionate power of the engines and consumption of fuel may be reduced.'

With this in mind, the GWSSCo building committee selected William Paterson to make their first ship. With his partner, John Mercer, he had had experience of building many ships in Bristol and was known 'as a man open to conviction, and not prejudiced in favour of either quaint or old-fashioned notions in ship building'. The keel of the *Great Western* was laid down in June 1836—at 206 ft. the longest ever seen—and work went on steadily for a year to put together what was probably the strongest merchant ship made up to that time. Brunel reported that her bottom was made entirely of oak. 'She is,' he said, 'most firmly and closely trussed with iron and wooden diagonals and shelf-pieces which, with the whole of her upper works, are fastened with screws and nuts to a much greater extent than has hitherto been put into practice.'

The launching on 19 July 1837 was modest in comparison with the *Great Britain*'s just five years later. Captain Claxton smashed a bottle of madeira over the bows as Mrs Miles named the ship. Some 50,000 cheered as she ran down the slipway at Bristol's Wapping, and the company directors gave a banquet for 300 an hour or so later in the safely moored hull. The engines had been made in London by Maudslay, Son & Field and the *Great Western* sailed round under her schooner rig with square topsail, and course on the foremast arriving at Gravesend after four days on 22 August to have them fitted.

Trials began in March 1838 and at the same time announcements appeared in the newspapers of her intended first sailing to America in April. She was to be a one class ship with room for 148 passengers at 35 guineas each, and 200 tons of cargo at £5 a ton. The Thames was a bit on the small side for testing so large a ship and she damaged a barge on one occasion and ran aground—for only half an hour—on another. On her run back to Bristol the *Great Western* caught fire when insulating boiler-felt near the funnel blazed up and so terrified four stokers that they took to a boat and rowed ashore near Leigh in Essex. Brunel, investigating, narrowly escaped death when he fell into the boiler room.

Alarm about Brunel, who was rushed ashore, proved misplaced. Alarm about the ship, when news of the mishap spread, was more serious and an estimated 50 intending passengers cancelled their tickets leaving a brave seven, including one woman, aboard for the maiden voyage. A small burden for such a big ship—the *Great Western* was 236 ft. overall, 31 ft. 9 in. wide, and weighed 1,230 gross tons. She had cost around £53,000, including £13,500 for the engines. Big as she was, Brunel had wanted her bigger—'from 400 to 500 tons larger than was eventually determined on, but the directors influenced by the doubts expressed by Mr Paterson as to her stability decided upon leaving the increase of size to their second ship.'

When the GWSSCo decided to go ahead and build an Atlantic steamer a little of their confidence rubbed off on to groups in Liverpool and London. In London the British and American Steam Navigation Company was founded and it ordered from builders in Limehouse the *British Queen*, a slightly larger vessel than the *Great Western*. Her builders made a big effort, but when the engine-making company went bankrupt, the company decided to hire the *Sirius* which operated between London and Cork. In Liverpool the Transatlantic Steamship Company made no attempt to have a ship of their own ready for 1838 but hired another, later, *Royal William*, built in 1836 for the Liverpool –Dublin run. This arrangement—whatever its precise details were—has left the City of Dublin Steam Packet Company with the credit and glory of owning the smallest passenger steamer ever to cross the Atlantic.

Though denied their own ship, the London contenders for the first Atlantic Blue Riband made sure that the *Sirius* was off to a good start. She was only about half the size (703 gross tons) of the *Great Western* and she left London on 28 March for a scheduled coaling stop at Cork while the *Great Western* was still undergoing trials. She left Cork on 4 April with 40 passengers and ran into a storm during which her skipper, Lt R. Roberts, RN, resisted demands that he put back. The bad weather delayed the *Great Western* a day and she left on 8 April. The *Sirius* pressed on under as big a head of steam as she could raise; some accounts say she burnt furniture and woodwork and took on 50 tons of coal from the New York pilot station, while others say she had left 15 of the 400 tons of coal she took on in Cork. In either case it was a close call; she did the voyage in 18 days 10 hours beating the *Great Western* by 3½ hours. The New York Irish were delighted.

The real achievement rested with the *Great Western* which crossed in 15 days 5 hours using 457 tons of coal (of 600 carried) and averaging 8.75 knots (the *Sirius* averaged 6.7 knots). The *Sirius* established that the Atlantic could be crossed non-stop by steam, and the Great Western company announced that it could be done comfortably and with a promise of regularity. It was left to the *Royal William* (175 ft. long and 276 horsepower) to stake Liverpool's belated claim as a transatlantic launching pad; she left on 5 July 1838 and as she went down the Mersey she in her turn proved how very nearly right Dr Lardner could have been. The *Royal William* was 'so deeply laden with coal for fuel—coal that filled her bunkers, her holds, and even her welldeck, that her paddles were buried six feet, her sponsons [platform linking paddle guard to deck] were submerged, and it was possible by leaning over the bulwarks to wash one's hands in the water'.

The promise implicit in the *Great Western*'s maiden voyage was amply fulfilled. She crossed the Atlantic 90 times for the GWSSCo carrying 4,318 passengers to America, returning with over 3,300. But making a profit was a very different matter. The dramatic shortfall between return and expectation in early steamships is easily illustrated. The *Great Western* cost £43 per gross ton to build compared with about £15 per ton for a sailing ship so that, allowing for the much greater amount of work she could do, the steamship cost at least half as much again as a sailer. All the space in a sailing ship's hull could be used to carry paying freight. The *Great Western* had room for only 200 tons of cargo, while space for 800 tons of coal was provided—

space not earning any revenue, but actually wasting the owners' substance shifting coal across the ocean. In addition, the engine room and its ancillaries filled half the hull space, and the company had to pay wages to extra categories of seamen—the engineer, the stoker and their assistants, the coal trimmers. The *Great Western* listed 52 total complement on her maiden voyage including ten seamen, five engineers, ten stokers, and eight trimmers.

R. H. Thornton in his excellent book *British Shipping* gives a table based on calculations made for the *Britannia*, Cunard's first ship. The result shows that in comparison with a sailing ship the steamer came out £2,550 worse off from a return trip over the Atlantic.

The impact of having only seven paying passengers on the *Great Western*'s first run must have brought home to the GWSSCo the size of the losses it would be possible to make. But on 7 November 1838 a lifeline was thrown out which the GWSSCo took more than a month to grab. The Government invited, in an advertisement, tenders from companies willing to carry mail across the Atlantic. The GWSSCo said that it would do the job but would need 18 months to two years to prepare its ships, which would have to be 1,200 tons register if built of wood, 200 less if of iron. For £45,000 a year it was prepared to undertake monthly crossings from England to Halifax providing the contract could be for seven years.

This offer was rejected. No reasons for the refusal were given. One suspects that the advertisement's purpose was to see what kind of offer would be forthcoming and to provide the Government—which had only its Peninsular experience to go on—with an idea of the terms in which it would have to think if a transatlantic contract were to be given. The GWSSCo, no doubt finding the going harder than it expected, fell to memorialising the Government frequently.

The whole rather sad story is in the minutes of the 1846 Parliamentary Select Committee on the Boston and Halifax Mails, which looked into the granting of the first mail contract to Samuel Cunard in 1840 on the occasion of Cunard moving down from Halifax and Boston to the GWSSCo's terminal port of New York. The inquiry provided a fine platform for the outlooks of the two contenders, Claxton and Cunard.

A memorial sent to Sir Robert Peel, the Prime Minister, on

26 May 1846, and quoted to the committee, sets out the GWSSCo position clearly. 'Your memorialists have, since 1842, carried on their trade with New York in their *Great Western* as well as they have been able, experience having proved that at times a larger ship would suffice and would have offered a better chance of remuneration, they have sent to sea the well-known iron ship *Great Britain*, which, acting under the advice of their engineer (Mr Brunel), they determined should be fitted with a screw propeller when that mode of propelling ships was quite in its infancy. She is now on her third voyage and your memorialists have every reason to believe that it will on all scientific points be successful. They did hope that they were about to reap a fair return for their outlay and enterprise but they have recently learned that arrangements are about to be made with the Halifax company [Cunard] to double the number of voyages for which they originally contracted and that New York is to be the rendezvous.

'Your memorialists believe that they have reason to complain of the very great injustice with which they have been treated from the commencement of the Government contract through which a sum far beyond £2½ million per annum is now paid to private companies not one of which would probably even by this time have had the opportunity for taking the contracts for transatlantic mails they have been so fortunate to obtain but for the success of the *Great Western*. If, however, the measure to which they allude is completed without compensation to your memorialists and the company they represent to the full extent of the injury which would be inflicted upon them, or giving them a chance to tender for the work, they hesitate not to say that so great an act of injustice was never before committed, and that the heavy hand of no previous Government ever pressed so heavily on a private enterprise that more deserved Government support.'

Petitioning Lord John Russell, the new Prime Minister, two months later, in July 1846, the GWSSCo say that extending Cunard's mail carrying contract into New York will create 'a complete monopoly of the steamship traffic between England and North America, which must end in the utter ruin of the GWSSCo and the consequent removal of all competition now most materially increased by the addition of their second ship the *Great Britain*'. The letter recalls the misfortune of the GWSSCo in not being awarded the mail contract in 1839 and says 'they, upon finding how great was the falling off of their receipts through the patronage of the Government, waited upon the Lords of the Treasury in February 1842' ... to no avail. This petition, too, ends in a flourish on the badness of extending Cunard's subsidy as 'inconsistent with public policy and repressive of private enterprise by confirming the principle of monopoly on one of the most important lines of passenger traffic between this and any other country, and which but for the exertions of your memorialists would still have been in the possession of the ships of the United States'.

'In consequence of receiving the refusal of the Government to give you any compensatory remuneration you determined,' Captain Claxton was asked during the Select Committee hearing, 'upon building the *Great Britain* steamship?' 'We determined upon building a ship that would carry double the number of passengers and double the quantity of freight.' 'You found it perfectly possible to go on with the *Great Western* steamship against the competition with Mr Cunard backed by Government money?' 'We found our returns very much decreased, of course, but we were obliged to go on even though loss was staring us in the face.' 'Would you have gone on supposing those vessels to have gone to New York instead of to Halifax and Boston?' 'I should say certainly not; we could not at that time have gone on.' 'Could you go on at the present time if they were to go to New York?' 'I do not think we could: not after the new line of vessels ran to New York.'

Questioned about the effect of competition on fares, Captain Claxton said: 'We began at £40 originally and when the *British Queen* began to run against us [first voyage 12 July 1839] they started at £45 and we went up, but we very soon reduced to £35, and then when we found the number of passengers that Mr Cunard's vessels were taking from us we came down to £30 in the *Great Western*.' 'In the *Great Britain* what do you charge?' 'We have many at £20, a good many at £30, and some at £25, the average being about £25.' All that the GWSSCo received from the Government was payment *pro rata* for letters and dispatches. Letters earned 2d. each going out but—the shipper fixing his own rate for the return trip—American letters to England were carried for a quarter of a dollar.

Captain Claxton gave the Committee details of transatlantic costs. 'For the first two years it was as near £1 a mile as could

The launching of the SS *Great Britain* at Bristol, 29 July, 1843. *National Maritime Museum*

The *Great Britain* being fitted out at Bristol, 1844. Believed to be the earliest photograph of a steamship. *National Maritime Museum*

SS *Great Britain* in 1845, in her original condition with six masts and one funnel.
National Maritime Museum

SS *Great Britain* after her first refit in 1846, reduced to five masts. *The Science Museum*

The *Great Britain* ashore at Dundrum, Ireland, in 1846, with the tide out. *From an oil painting in the Science Museum*

Ashore at Dundrum, with the tide in. *From an oil painting in the Science Museum*

Salvaging the *Great Britain* in 1847—with the aid of James Bremner's sand-filled boxes, and other lifting devices. *Radio Times Hulton Picture Library*

The *Great Britain* with four masts and two funnels, 1852-6. *National Maritime Museum*

SS Great Britain with three masts and one funnel, 1856–75. *National Maritime Museum*

Officers of the SS *Great Britain* at the beginning of her Australian period. Uniforms for merchant navy officers were just being introduced. Captain Barnard Mathews is seated in the centre with F. P. Smith, who pioneered the use of the screw propeller, standing behind, hands clasped. *State Library of Victoria, Australia*

Captain John Gray, master of the *Great Britain* for 18 years, with a typical testimonial from his passengers. He disappeared mysteriously in 1872. *State Library of Victoria, Australia*

SS *Great Britain* in the Thames on her last voyage to Australia in 1875.
National Maritime Museum

The *Great Britain* in San Francisco, probably in 1882. This is the only known photograph of her as a sailing ship. *San Francisco Maritime Museum*

The *Great Britain* anchored in Port Stanley in 1905 as a wool hulk for the Falkland Island Co. *The Science Museum*

The *Great Britain* aground in Sparrow Cove before her recovery.
Great Britain Project

Another view of the *Great Britain* in Sparrow Cove. *Great Britain
Project*

Dr Ewan Corlett at Avonmouth on the return of the *Great Britain*, June 1970. *Topix*

The *Great Britain* passing under Clifton Suspension Bridge (another of Brunel's masterpieces) on her way up the River Avon to Bristol, June 1970.

A view of the *Great Britain* back in the Great Western Dock.

Safely back, after 127 years, in the Bristol dry dock where she was built. Clearly seen here as white on the hull are the remnants of the zinc sheeting placed up to the 25-ft mark over the 1882 3½ inch pitch pine cladding.

The *Great Britain*'s winches.

Plywood patches over the upper part of the great crack on the starboard side of the ship, started from a hole cut to transship wool bales in the Falklands.

No echo here of the Arabesque pilasters, the gilded doors, or the delicate lemon tints of the 1845 decor; looking forward from just behind the mizzen mast position in 1970 only the skeleton of the vessel remains.

High pressure steam being used to clean 85 years' accumulated marine growth from the *Great Britain*'s hull in the Great Western Dock, Bristol. The sealed-off propeller tube can be seen clearly. *The Guardian*

be. But from that time it has gradually been getting less and less by economy and more attention to the arrangements till now I think we go from England to New York and back in the *Great Western* for £4,100 or £4,200; you may call it about 14s. or 15s. a mile.' [Cunard's 1970 costs per mile.] These costs included all seagoing costs and harbour and other dues, but not depreciation or interest on capital. Fares out and home varied. 'Fares out by the *Great Western* are £30, and by the *Great Britain* £20, £25, and £30. Ours home are £20. 16s. 8d. by the *Great Western*—it comes out this way because it is a calculation of dollars—the *Great Britain* is £16.'

At the outset cargo charges on the *Great Western* were £5 a ton, but in 1843 it went to £7 a ton. The goods sent were all lightweight—'goods for a rapid market, if they are not sold at the moment some of them come back again, and the manufacturer would as cheerfully pay £10 a ton to get the goods out in the short time that the ship is upon the Atlantic as £7—they never dispute it, though by the liners they give £2 showing the importance they attach to the difference between a rapid return of money and the goods lying aboard a ship an uncertain time'. The £5-per-ton rate lasted until the GWSSCo transferred its business to Liverpool. 'The principal part of our goods came from the North, Scotland, and Lancashire. When we sailed from Bristol they had not only to bear our freight but the land freight. At Liverpool, which is the great emporium of Manchester goods, they have not to bear that freight.' And the trade was all exports; the charge per ton eastbound over the Atlantic was between 30s. and £2—'it is hardly worth taking on board'.

Invited by the committee to interpret the views of his supporters, Captain Claxton said: 'They feel that if competition is destroyed the rate of passengers fares and the rate of freight of goods will be greatly increased. No line of packets can maintain a competition against a line that is paid at the rate of £4,000 a voyage for carrying the mails. In the wintertime when it is very essential that a communication should be kept up, it will not pay them at all to go if they are not put upon the same footing as mail packets are put upon. The memorialists fear that if the vessels cannot go the whole year round it will end in the establishment of only one company which they greatly deprecate. They object to one company having £4,000 per voyage. They wish all companies to be put on an equal footing as regards the payment from the public, and if the public pays for services done, they think the payment for services should be equally divided amongst all English companies.'

This seems an equitable stance. That it failed to convince has to be seen in the light of the clever performance Samuel Cunard put on for the Committee in the strange role of a man reluctantly saddled with a Government subsidy for the thankless task of running a line of steamers—a task he is always on the verge of abandoning because of the meanness of his backers. Backers who, incidentally, increased the taxpayer's contribution to his turnover from £55,000 in 1839 to £145,000 a year in 1846. Disclaiming all knowledge of the advertisement for an Atlantic mail service, Cunard came to England in the winter of 1839, 'with the view expressly of trying whether I could induce the Government to enter into some arrangement with myself by which that mode of [transatlantic] communication might be much improved.... I came to England to point out to the Government that an American line was about being got up and I wished to prevent it, and that it would therefore be in the interests of this Government to assist me in carrying it out.' Cunard was the son of an immigrant in Pennsylvania who moved to Canada in retreat from American independence, so his patriotic motive may be respected.

His plan, he told Treasury officials, 'would save the Government the sum they had spent for the old packets which was about £40,000 a year besides the loss of hundreds of lives annually and that I would produce as much postage as the sum I asked. And I have proved that more money has been received for postage than has been paid to me besides the saving of £40,000 a year and the substitution of a safe and speedy communication twice a month for the uncertain and dangerous communication of once a month as formerly. The plan was entirely my own and the public have the advantage of it.' It had been a hard struggle; the original £55,000 subsidy crept to £80,000 by 1841 when another £10,000 a year was asked—'for additional work?' Cunard was asked. 'It was not for additional work, but for that additional sum we should have given up the contract. Up to that time trade was very bad and there was a good deal of competition. We had competing with us the *British Queen* and the *Great Western* and we found we were unable to go on.'

Pressed about the injustice of his having been given contracts from 1839 to 1846 without competition—was it not 'a mere matter of favour?' 'No, I do not think it is a matter of favour,' Cunard answered, 'I think the Government have not used me well by not giving me enough.' Giving the mail contract to New York to anybody else would 'virtually be bringing a line in competition with me. I call my line the Government line and therefore I say they could not do that.' He noted that in that very day's paper it said that the Americans had signed a contract for a State-aided line—could he keep going with even £145,000 a year against Collins and the GWSSCo? 'It is very questionable; indeed in my correspondence I have had with the Government I have stated that in my opinion we shall hardly be able to do it. It depends upon increased trade between the two countries.' How much worse, must the position of the GWSSCo have seemed.

Cunard had no doubt about it—could it keep going? 'I cannot imagine that they can ... by their own showing they are in a very bad way, and have been for years.... I do not think they can continue the line.... I think they never had any profits.... Two or three years ago they applied to us to know whether we could give them a certain sum of money if they would remove their vessels off the line. We did not entertain it at all because we say we will carry on our work irrespective of anybody else.' Even if the GWSSCo had been in good shape it could not, Cunard felt, have kept going without a subsidy from mails. Its only advantages, in his view, were that 'they may choose their time ... fix the days of starting at periods of the year as they choose and to suit their interest ... in the spring of the year they give a little detail of what they mean to do, and for the last four or five years they have never had a winter voyage. We are compelled to go in the winter months therefore we should not have so many passengers per voyage as they would.'

Though dismissive of the GWSSCo's prospects, Cunard acknowledged that the arrival of the *Great Britain* on station in 1845 made him bring down his fares—'38 guineas and a guinea for the steward'. It was done while he was in Halifax, however, and he regretted it. 'It will not be done again. I thought it looked like an opposition which I was sorry to see.' Cunard seems to draw no comfort from the ramshackle state of his competitors, starting with the ruin after only two years' working of the British and American Steam Navigation Company with losses, he estimated, of £100,000. These show how crucial the mail contract was, and this well-prepared reply indicates how important Cunard thought it to impress the committee. It asked: 'If you had possession of the field to New York as the *Great Western* is now in possession of it would you not consider yourself ill-used if you had been excluded from competition for the Government tender?'

'I do not think I should,' said Cunard. 'I would illustrate it in this way. When we took this contract the GWSSCo were in possession of the port of Bristol. It was stated that Bristol was the nearest port to sail from, and the most favourable (I speak from their own papers); the *British Queen* and the *President* were in possession of the Port of London, and I was therefore obliged to go to Liverpool. As soon as I got myself established there down comes the *Great Western* and cuts me out. I do not complain of it, but they took the goods and passengers from me. I consider that they had a right to come to Liverpool as much as I have a right to go to New York.' Would a joint service be a fair compromise? 'I would not have entered into a joint contract with anybody upon any conditions whatever for I do not think it could have been carried out.'

Captain Claxton was recalled before the committee and asked 'Will you have the goodness to explain the transaction alluded to by Mr Cunard of some proposal for selling the *Great Western* steamship?' 'Between two and three years ago we were endeavouring to sell the *Great Western* at the request of our proprietors and in opposition to the wish of the directors, to the Peninsular and Orient company, and a bargain was well-nigh concluded and we then, before it was completed, engaged Mr Ashton a shipbroker to negotiate with Mr Cunard's agents at Liverpool to get a small sum for taking her off the line. The P & O did not offer us a sum within £3/4,000 of what we considered her worth, but we were pressed by our proprietors and we endeavoured to get that difference, I think it was either £3,000 or £4,000 from Messrs MacIver who are agents for Mr Cunard as a bonus to us to take her out of their way. But we had the *Great Britain* coming on at the time.'

On 3 August 1846 the committee reported that Cunard was doing a good job, regretted that the GWSSCo had suffered from the tenders not being competitive and 'considering the meritorious character of the services rendered by the latter company and its priority of establishment on the New York line will be glad if, on any future extension of the Royal Mail service it receives the favourable consideration of the Government'. Would the recommendation have been stronger in favour of the GWSSCo if Captain Claxton had handed up fewer memorials and urged the prudence, as well as the justice, of State help for a company that had pioneered in two vessels a technical revolution? With the promise of a mail subsidy, would the GWSSCo have built a second *Great Britain* and established a regular pattern of three week sailings? Having failed to build four or five *Great Westerns* in 1839-41 and set themselves up on a firm basis, the company was probably by this stage too demoralised to take any fresh initiative. Six weeks after the committee reported, the *Great Britain* went aground at Dundrum and debates about the recovery of the GWSSCo at once became academic.

Samuel Cunard was almost certainly correct in saying that the GWSSCo encountered difficulties very early in its history—difficulties from which he removed any prospect of relief when he secured the mail contract. The select committee recommended that the GWSSCo receive a share of any extension of the mail subsidy. Help was indeed on its way, adding a poignant twist to the tail of the story. Having failed to win even part of the transatlantic mail contract the GWSSCo had decided to put the *Great Britain* on the emigrant trade to Sydney, Australia. The Chancellor of the Exchequer promised that if this service was established the state would give the GWSSCo the same amount per voyage (£3,295) to Australia as Cunard received for each trip to America.

But for many GWSSCo shareholders there had already been too many 'ifs'—their repeated insistence on winding up the company makes this clear. Their company had pioneered, against the obscurantism of the dock board, and had been rebuffed by a Government that should have given at least a little encouragement. They had had no rewards. All the original £100 shares were written off, and the loss on the building yard was £42,277. The total losses at the close exceeded £100,000. 'A disastrous ending,' said Charles Wells, 'of an enterprise that ought to have secured for Bristol supremacy in the North Atlantic trade.' It wasn't disastrous only for the Great Western Steam-Ship Company—exports from Bristol dropped in value from £339,728 in 1839, to £150,883 in 1846.

CHAPTER V

The Long Haul

After the dizzy heights and tearful depths of its beginning, the *Great Britain* story goes into a gloomy intermission in the autumn of 1847. After acclaim in New York and huzzas at Dundrum there is only the scurry of bailiffs' agents, the head shaking of the dock board rent collector, and the tap of the auctioneer's hammer. In April 1848 that hammer was knocking down the ship's furnishings and stores—970 sheets, 1,556 towels, 228 hair mattresses, 406 feather pillows, and much more. The *Great Britain* herself went up for auction in September with a reserve price of £40,000 on her; the bidding stopped at half that.

In June 1849 there was a strong rumour that the Collins Line had bought her for £20,000 and were about to spend £23,000 on renovation. Mr E. K. Collins, owner of the Dramatic trans-atlantic sailing line, had emerged as the founder in 1849 of the heavily-subsidised fleet of super steamships with which the Americans aimed to 'neutralise' the British monopoly in steam. Congressman Bayard clamoured for the United States to 'enter the contest with England for the supremacy of ocean steam navigation'. Not to try would, he said, 'ensure national disappointment more deeply felt from the fact that England has already been vanquished by our sailing ships, and gracefully yielded to us the palm of victory'.

'We must have speed, extraordinary speed,' he went on, to catch up with or escape from any other ship. The super vessels 'must be fit for the purpose of a cruiser with armament to attack your enemy (if that enemy were Great Britain) in her most vital part—her commerce'. Perhaps the name of Brunel's ship stuck in the Collins Line craw. More likely, for the name could easily have been changed, the iron construction put that company off. It opted for old-fashioned wood for its mighty (3,000 tons register) ships; they *were* fast and knocked 14 hours 23 minutes off average Cunard timings. But two ships sank, and in seven years

such stupendous losses had been made, even with a mail subsidy three times that enjoyed by Cunard, that the Collins Line
collapsed. The *Great Britain* might have been too demure for
it—for as Mr Thornton said, 'the Collins Line ... did at least
light a candle of decorative vulgarity which in many of our
larger passenger ships is burning brightly to the present day'.
Collins ships had steam central heating.

Rejected by the Americans, the *Great Britain* lay wanly in
Clarence Dock. In 1850 there is only one item of news—suitably
funereal—which was the death of a Mr William Frith who fell
over the side and drowned on 29 July. His descendants are still
wondering what he was doing there. It is quite likely that the
GWSSCo had reverted yet again to its stand-by device of charg-
ing to look over the *Great Britain*. But debts—for the ship's
berth—kept accumulating and as a last, seemingly desperate,
measure the *Great Britain* was sold for £18,000 to Gibbs, Bright
and Co. This was scarcely a radical change for the ship. Robert
Bright in Bristol, and his partner in London, George Gibbs, were
leading spirits in the foundation of the Great Western Railway
of which they, and George's brother Henry, became directors.
The first meeting of the Bristol and London Railway promoting
committees took place in Gibbs, Bright's parent company offices
in London. So although not involved directly in the GWSSCo's
establishment, Gibbs, Bright & Co then 27 years old, had in-
timate links with it. As shipping agents they ran GWSSCo
affairs in Liverpool where the Bright side of the firm had had a
branch office since 1805.

The company was involved with the Eagle line of sailing
packets, but the *Great Britain* was its first venture in steam. To
get her ready for sea the estimate from Fawcett, Preston & Co
was £15,886 for the hull and rigging and another £5,808 for
the engines. The bill in the end was almost certainly greater
because Gibbs, Bright brought up William Paterson to super-
vise the work, and the firm decided to fit a new engine made by
John Penn of Greenwich. Apart from never having eliminated
its teething troubles, the original engine had sustained the
greatest damage at Dundrum. The new engine was designed to
work at ten pounds per square inch (compared with four lb. for
its predecessor). And instead of filling a third of the ship, the
new engine room was only 78.4 ft. long and very much more compact. The first engine room was 116.8 ft. long and occupied 1,919

tons of space, compared with 1,475 tons after 1852.

As well as being more compact, the new twin 88½-in. cylinder oscillating engine was more efficient. It was rated at 500 horse-power, but 800 horsepower was claimed for it as an indicated rating. Instead of the four-chain drive it reverted to four cogs, still giving three revolutions of the propeller to one of the crank shaft.

Instead of lying fore and aft, the new boilers ran across the ship and were fired through nine furnace doors—three per boiler—on each side of the ship. This firing system resulted in the novelty of two side-by-side funnels. As the models Brunel showed to Queen Victoria suggested, the next screw was a three-bladed version, still 15 ft. 6 in. in diameter. This new combina-tion produced the elusive ten knots without difficulty. By replacing the two aftermost schooner-sail masts with a single mast similarly rigged the number of masts went down to four, carrying 300 square yards of canvas; still eluding 'nautical cognomen' the *Great Britain* at this time achieved (in my view) her best proportions.

From the changes described so far it is not certain what pur-pose Gibbs, Bright had in mind for the ship. The addition of a long deckhouse—stretching over 250 ft. from the stern to just beyond the foremast—almost doubled the previous passenger capacity to 730, of whom only 50 were to be first class. This points to the emigrant trade, the better end of it perhaps, then running at unparalleled levels as the despairing Irish evacuated their famine-ridden and oppressed island. Captain Claxton thought that the new owners intended to use the *Great Britain* on the transatlantic service. The new commander continued the GWSSCo connection; Captain Barnard Mathews had been an officer on the *Great Western*, and more recently master of the *City of Glasgow* on the run to Philadelphia. He took the *Great Britain* from Liverpool for America on 1 May 1852 and arrived after a passage of 13 days 7 hours, returning almost at once.

All steam-ships on the Atlantic station at this time—and for 30 years to come—carried sails. But the sails were already, and would increasingly become, the emergency source of power. On the Australian run sails were the chief motive power and the engines were used for getting the ship through the calms ten degrees each side of the Equator, and against head winds. The great distance, poor machinery, insufficient room for coal, and few coaling stations, were the reasons why steam remained only an auxiliary to sail until the Suez Canal and better engineering made their effects felt in the 1870s. But with an 800 horsepower engine capable of pushing her at ten knots, the *Great Britain* could qualify as both an Atlantic steamer as well as an Australian auxiliary. Maybe Gibbs, Bright intended to use her as a single all-purpose fast ship which, without timetable obligations, could snatch up the best trading opportunities as they occurred.

Debates about the *Great Britain*'s employment—if there were any—ended decisively when incredible rumours from Australia that there had been huge findings of gold were confirmed. The state of the sailing ship connection to that remote and flavourless colony—often a six-month voyage away—explains why the great discoveries of 1851 were not widely appreciated until about the middle of 1852. The effect was immediate—demand for berths rocketed. Three steamers were able to take advantage straightaway of the urgent need of prospectors to be in Australia as soon as possible: the *Chusan* auxiliary which opened the P & O mail service to Australia, the *Australia*, belonging to the Australian Royal Mail Steam Navigation Company, and the *Great Britain*. Brunel's ship had started what was to be almost her life's work during which she contributed largely to changing Australia from an anaemic version of England into a country with a character of its own.

Gold was what gave this change impetus. It had been discovered several times before. Once, in 1828, a convict found a big nugget near Bathurst. The officer in charge of the work party immediately flogged him on the presumption that he had stolen the gold and melted it down. In 1841 the Rev W. B. Clarke showed the governor some gold that he had found. 'Put it away, Mr Clarke,' he was told, 'or we shall all have our throats cut.' These and other fearful kinds of suppression lost their edge when gold was found in California in 1848. The Government stopped trying to pretend gold was not there, and appointed a surveyor to look for it.

Most of the early finds were in New South Wales—flour prices rose in Sydney from £20 to £70 a ton at the diggings. Just as New South Wales disliked losing population to America, so Victoria disliked losing its citizens to its northern neighbour and it set up a gold discovery committee in Melbourne offering

£200 for news of a mine within 200 miles of Melbourne. By August 1851 the beginnings of the Ballarat field were uncovered and in December Henry Frenchman revealed 'what seemed to be the inexhaustible riches of Bendigo'. Whole suburbs and towns emptied of men, leaving women to form communes for protection. Governor C. J. Latrobe of Victoria reported the wholesale desertions: 'Farmers and respectable agriculturists have found that the only way, as those employed by them deserted, was to leave their farms, join them, and form a band and go shares; but even masters of vessels forseeing the impossibility of maintaining any control over their men otherwise have made up parties among them to do the same.' Only two policemen remained in Melbourne and 50 London police were sent out as replacements.

Finds were sometimes prodigious. One man dug out 80 lb. of gold in a day; another filled a quart pot with ore in a day equipped only with a pen-knife. These were exceptional; the best arrangement was found to be a working party of four and they could on average expect to find between them an ounce of gold a day. Extravagance naturally followed—horses were shod with golden shoes, and the riot of riches at diggers' weddings was reported to be almost incredible. Lady Denison complained that there was no longer a division between rich and poor even as far away as Hobart. Ancillary trades did well—a destitute lollipop seller opened a bar on the road to Ballarat and made £6,000 a year.

One expected effect that the gold finds did not produce was civil disorder, or even much throat-cutting. They did knock the last nail in the coffin of transportation—stopped by order in council in 1840—for the resumption of which there had been some pressure. The chief consequences of the Australian gold rush were naturally economic, and they had a crucial bearing on shipping. First, the population exploded; in the ten years 1840–50 Government assisted emigration increased the Australian population by 215,000, while in the next ten years the increase was 3½ times as great. To Victoria in 1852 alone 50,000 came from overseas; by 1858 there were more people in Victoria than in the whole of Australia six years before. In the decade after 1850 it was easier to produce gold to buy imports abroad than it was to make anything—except perhaps refined sugar— at home. Ships came to the country laden with cargo as well as migrants. In addition to freeing Australia from total dependence on wool, gold paradoxically helped the wool trade by allowing it to be sent to England much more cheaply, and without any need for it to be compressed and damaged. Ships' holds were waiting to be filled with any cargo that could be found. Cargoes were derivative; people were the prime movers and the simple commercial star followed by Gibbs, Bright was that £124 millions in gold discoveries produced a growth in population from 405,000 in 1851 to 1,100,000 by 1861.

The *Great Britain* was as fast off the mark in the gold-rush traffic as anybody. She sailed on 21 August 1852 from Liverpool with 615 passengers (8 first class), a crew of 137, and more than £7,000 of food and drink aboard. The voyage was uneventful until the ship was well on towards the Cape of Good Hope, where it was due to call. On 18 September the log entry reads: 'Saturday: strong gales and squally high sea on; several seas struck ship heavily, a high topping sea breaking over at times. Nine a.m.: Consultation held by Captain Mathews and his chief and second officers, chief engineer, also H. Thorp and Captain Underwood, passengers. Deciding it was imprudent to proceed at 10 a.m. the ship's head was turned to north-west for St Helena and all sail made. Now 236 miles from African coast, 1,036 miles from St Helena, 723 from Table Bay. Ship has made no progress for two days, also light and high out of the water. Every appearance of continued severe weather. Valuable ship and cargo including specie (coins) valued £1 million—signed Barnard R. Mathews, comr.: H. T. Cox, C.O.; John Gray, S.O.; J. Cannon, C.E.; H. Thorp; E. Underwood, passenger.' The usual reason put forward for this long trek back to St Helena is that the *Great Britain* was running short of coal; Mr Cannon's presence at the conference suggests that this was a factor. But it is odd that the log does not mention this reason for turning round. It cannot have been a popular decision with the eager diggers. After a call at Cape Town, the ship arrived in Melbourne on 12 November—a slow passage of 82 days.

Both the send-off from Liverpool and the welcome in Australia were on as grand a scale as for the maiden voyage to America. There was a greater element of suspicion about this longer journey through less familiar seas—the *Great Britain* carried six heavy guns and arms and ammunition for 100 men.

On both her first two trips to Australia, the *Great Britain*

went on from Melbourne to complete the 588 miles to Sydney
—almost certainly there was enough interstate movement by
gold-diggers to make this short hop pay. On her maiden voyage
she came back to England via South Africa because coaling
facilities had not yet been set up along the Cape Horn route
which was later invariably used for the homeward run. She
arrived in Liverpool in April 1853.

Among those who travelled on the *Great Britain*—but never
arrived—were: two Oxen, one Milking Cow, 30 Pigs, 150 Sheep,
two Lambs, one Calf, 56 Turkeys and Geese, 250 Ducks, 550
Fowls. This list is from the ship's inventory for a voyage home
from Australia; there was a butcher on board to kill and prepare
the meat for the saloon, and his was an important department.
'We fancy sometimes we are in a farm yard,' wrote an emigrant,
'for there are pigs, and sheep, geese and hens, altogether in a
boat; they make a great noise but they look dirty and unhappy.'
Lifeboats were commonly used for holding the smaller animals
and it was argued that they could quickly be tipped out if the
need arose.

Apart from this feature common to all long voyages in the
middle of the last century, the *Great Britain* was in nearly all
respects a better and more comfortable ship than her competitors. She rolled heavily, and you could nail your belongings on
the wall, but otherwise there is a feeling that she was not too
different from a day trip to the Isle of Man multiplied by 60.
The *Great Britain* is about the size of a Manx ferry boat. But
to see how exceptional she was, it is necessary to look at the
run-of-the-mill shipping environment of the time. And at some
of the pressures and arguments that contributed to that environment.

More than anything else in the 1850s—when a major inquiry,
the second in ten years, was held into excessive deaths at sea—
the lavatory exercised the minds of port officials and humani-
tarians. Sometimes they were put up in the bows, little cabins
with a hole in the floor, which got washed overboard when the
first green sea went over the ship; women avoided them because
they were too near the crew. Sometimes they were in the stern.
'But the great objection is,' the chief emigration officer at Liverpool said, 'that the captain would be obliged to have this annoyance under his nose or eyesight.' So on the Australian run, the
1854 enquiry was told, 'We have generally put four amidships,

but they have been found to be so great a nuisance that we have proposed to remove all but two, one in the female hospital, and one for the single women and to put all the others on deck.

'But they hardly ever get to Australia without being out of order. In the first place the working of the ship deranges them, and then the people who are put aboard are not in the habit of using that kind of convenience and they use it very ill, and throw bones and all sorts of things down it. They are the greatest nuisance that can possibly be aboard ship. I believe on board men-of-war they are bad enough, and they are much worse aboard emigrant ships. It is almost impossible to prevent their leaking. The people do not understand the plugs and they every now and then set the water going and do not turn it off and then they flood the decks. We have now tried to get them self-acting, but a thing that works very well on shore as self-acting will not act at sea. In fact I confess we are at our wits' end on the subject of water closets.'

Wits were wracked to try to get an answer. Complicated arrangements for separating and dispatching 'soil and liquid by different holes' failed. In ships chartered by the Government for carrying emigrants overhead cisterns were introduced and made standard with a device to operate the cistern 'when the closet is stepped into'. Others chose a scheme—'the same as they have in railway stations'—where the movement of the door actuated the water, but it was found to be too complicated and did not work. The effect of half-baked equipment, unfamiliarity with water closets in any form by prospective users, and the indifference and extra mess resulting from sea sickness was indescribable and intolerable. The death rate on emigrant ships to America in 1847 was over 17 per cent—exceptional because of the famine—but in 1852 it was 4.48 per cent going to Australia where American ships could not be blamed. But the running squalor between decks after the passengers had been battened down for a week's run before a gale could.

These poor people endured all this misery and danger to escape famine—after 1845—and to get rich quick—after 1851. These new reasons only added to the pressure put on the poor by the British Government which had been concerned ever since the end of the Napoleonic wars at the mysterious growth in population which was a stress in many ways, but chiefly upon the medieval poor law. The solution was complementary to the growth of Empire—export them. Propaganda was put out, not always with complete success, according to William Chambers. 'In the cottages throughout the most destitute parts of Ireland one may meet stuck on the walls as decorations the announce-ments of the Emigration Board or of the various associations devoted to the same object, but it is sadly clear that the inmates know little more of their practical meaning than if they were Chinese announcements on a tea chest.'

With the benefit of Captain Mathews' report on this voyage, Gibbs, Bright gave serious thought to the suitability of their ship for the job she now seemed likely to do for some time—carry on trade with Australia. Their thoughts concentrated on the four-masted rig first. Its justification was no stronger than that it was an improvement, from a handling point of view, over Brunel's six.

Five of Brunel's six masts had been dispensable, but Gibbs, Bright and Co was in the Australian trade where there was no hope of steaming all the way. The *Great Britain* would inevit-ably *sail* much of the way, often in heavy weather. Three square-rigged masts would provide more push than two square- and two schooner-rigged where, just looking at the pictures, the second mast if carrying full sail, must have screened the schooner sail on the foremast.

In the spring of 1853 Gibbs, Bright claimed that 'she has ... been rendered altogether independent of her engines by having been re-masted and rigged as a clipper sailing ship, for which her beautiful model is so remarkably adapted.'

Captain Mathews took the ship out for trials on 5 July and reported that she 'was put through all the manoeuvres of tacking and wearing while the screw was fixed and with perfect success with all the sail set ... showing her capability of carrying almost any amount of canvas that can by possibility be put upon her; with the engines averaging a speed of 18 revolutions a speed of $12\frac{1}{2}$ knots was attained; and if at that time circumstances had permitted of her being run to leeward, I have no kind of doubt whatever that she would have gone over 14 knots'. Commenting on detailed alterations, Gibbs, Bright said that 'in order to in-crease the effect of her steam power and remove the vibration common in screw steamers she has been fitted with Griffith's patent propeller, so successfully tried in Her Majesty's yacht'.

Encouraged by the captain's good report, Gibbs, Bright were prepared to back the ship with a wager. There was room for 300 tons of general cargo to be carried at £8 a ton—'40s. per ton to be forfeited by the ship should the passage from Liverpool lighthouse to Port Phillip Heads exceed 65 days'. The company proposed to reduce the number of passengers taken from the 600 plus taken first time to make life on board more tolerable. Premium fares were being charged: 70 guineas in the After-Saloon, 65 for Midship Berths, 42 in the Fore-Saloon (second class), 30 to 32 guineas in what was called Lower Cabin, and there were a few places tucked away in some unnamed corner at 25 guineas. Children under 14 and female servants went half price, manservants went at the lower cabin rate. Dogs £5 each. On any of the eight sailing clippers in which Gibbs, Bright had an interest the fares were £50 first class, £24-£30 second, and £20-£22 the rest.

For a first class fare it was promised that the after saloon 'will be found with a first rate table'. In the fore-saloon 'a plain substantial table will be provided'. But for both these groups 'every requisite will be provided including beds, berths, plate, bedding, linen'. Class distinctions were firmly imposed on areas of access. The poop aft was for after-saloon and midships passengers alone, the spar deck amidships for the first and fore-saloon passengers, and the forward part of the ship for lower cabin passengers. For those forward life was more regimented than elsewhere—'passengers will be formed into messes, and must assist the stewards', was the instruction. They were provided with two tin plates, one tin cup and saucer, one drinking cup, one knife and fork, two spoons, dishes, tea and coffee pots. Other requisites such as beds, bedding, towels, soap, blacking brushes 'must be laid in by the passengers'. Silver & Co in St George's Crescent, Liverpool, could supply these materials, Gibbs, Bright said, with the reminder that the berths were 6 ft. by 20 in. Far from having to struggle across Liverpool with his bed under his arm the first class passenger looked forward to the ease of smoking rooms (or ladies' boudoirs), baths, and music. In addition to all its previous 'firsts' the *Great Britain* claimed at this period to be the first ship with a piano on board —'wants tuning badly', said Edward Grace, W.G.'s brother, sailing out with the second English cricket test team in 1863.

This was the ship, newly rigged, with a propeller-tested-by-

royalty, retaining her rare parallel funnels that set out for Australia for the second time on 11 August 1853, arriving in
Melbourne on 25 October—66 days all told but just inside the
65 between Liverpool lighthouse and Port Phillip stipulated for
the start of the cargo penalty. A damned close run thing. The
return home via the Falklands—to which coal for the *Great
Britain* was especially shipped—was made in a creditable 62
days—Christmas Eve 1853 to 25 February 1854.

Having run the *Great Britain* in on the Australian route
Captain Mathews decided to retire from the sea and take up a
post in Australia as Lloyds agent. He was 50. He went out to
start his new job with his wife Mary and three sons (he had 12
children in all, but most died in infancy) on the next voyage
when he helped to run in the new master, John Gray aged 33.
The new captain was from the Shetlands. He first went to sea
in local fishing vessels before leaving the island to sail before
the mast on ships to America. He had worked his way up, after
eight years as a seaman, to be captain of the Gibbs, Bright ship
Eagle. His wife is said to have been put out when he decided
to join the *Great Britain* as second officer.

John Gray was extremely popular—perhaps the need to find
an outlet for this side of his character was what caused him to
leave the captain's cabin in small vessels for the more gregarious
life of a big liner. He was a most careful and punctilious man
who went through all the checks and drills. He was particularly
alert to fire risk and therefore strict about lights-out rules. When
there was ice about Captain Gray spent long miserable hours
on watch; when bad weather stretched the crew he was not
afraid to get hold of a rope himself and lend a hand—dishing
out a helping of grog to the crew after particularly gruelling
spells aloft. To the passengers he seems to have had a touch of
reassuring remoteness that combined well with—indeed enhanced—a cheery word which he readily exchanged when on his
rounds of the ship.

He pandered slightly to their fears, made them feel that they
and the captain had together braved unprecedented horrors. In
the Irish Sea gale of February 1861 'he had never had the *Great
Britain* out in such weather before'. Two years later there was a
storm as the ship approached her Australian destination and—
no pilot coming out, and the vessel drifting ashore—Captain
Gray piloted her through the Port Phillip Heads. His comment

afterwards was 'that to possess the whole of Australia he would not suffer so for two days'. Again the storm that sent the *Great Britain* into Holyhead at the start of her trip in December 1871 was 'the worst he had ever encountered'. The verdict in general was, in Edward Grace's phrase: 'Capital fellow, the captain.'

Competent, polite, and rather diffident, he was naturally a man around whom the Victorian ladies liked to flutter. In November 1863 he fell, 'looking up while passing the intermediate stairs', taking most of the skin off his nose and blacking both eyes. Next day he was too unwell to appear, but the ladies paid him a visit. The only particular attachment recorded is towards Rachel Henning whom, as she reports, he went out of his way to visit in England, and escorted diligently in Australia. A bracelet he gave her is still occasionally worn by her descendants in England.

That he had a sentimental streak and that he had become famous during his 18 years as captain of the *Great Britain*, at least in Australia, is shown by an incident in Melbourne during the visit to Australia of the first Duke of Edinburgh. At a 'panorama' [lantern slide] show the Duke's ship *Galatea* was shown followed by the *Great Britain* and Captain Gray. Gray was spotted in the audience. 'I can see the dear old captain,' runs a turn of the century reminiscence, 'tears in his eyes, waving his handkerchief from a seat in the stalls' in response to the cheers.

But the best way to achieve immortality as a nineteenth-century sea captain was to be American, or to be mistaken for an American. In the 1850s and on through the 60s the ascendancy established by the United States in sailing vessels—then being eroded by British steamers—was reflected in an American dominance in the mythology of the sea; they were the autocrats of the deep-sea ships. 'We had a captain,' an English traveller in an American ship told an inquiry, 'who whenever he chose to give you a blow with a rope or anything else would do so.' This kind of story much embroidered had laughable consequences, with ordinary British captains grafting on American accents— Sir William Runciman recalled asking for a job as a sailor: 'With a strangely mixed American and North Country vocabulary and accent the captain reminded me that he guessed the packet I was applying to sail in was above the standard of my training.' It was against men like these that Captain Gray found himself competing for trade.

His start as the master of the *Great Britain* was not auspicious. She left Liverpool on 28 April 1854 but put back again almost at once because of a serious defect in her new propeller fittings. This took six weeks to repair and the ship finally left on 12 June arriving in Melbourne after a sixty-seven-day voyage on 18 August. On the 22nd Captain Gray wrote to the *Melbourne Argus*: 'I am happy to state that I feel perfectly confident the *Great Britain* can make a direct passage from Liverpool to Melbourne without calling at any port; and do yet look forward to her making it under 60 days.'

His immediate problem was not speed but smallpox. Cases had been diagnosed on board and the ship was put in quarantine for three weeks. When this time was up, on the evening of 8 September, Captain Gray fired his cannon a few times and set off some rockets. The Crimean war had been declared in the spring and somebody on the *Argus* turned in a light piece the headline 'The Russians in the Bay'. It spoke of troops under arms for hours at the barracks and thousands going down to the waterfront to see the enemy land. 'This was a piece of exhilaration said the *Argus* which might well have been dispensed with. It threw the city and its suburbs into a great state of excitement.' There was a repeat performance when the ship fired a cannon to announce her arrival in the Mersey.

The war did catch up with the ship when she returned home —delayed by quarantine and the call at Sydney. The war was then a year old and the *Great Britain*, as one of the biggest vessels afloat, should have been commandeered at the outset. Had the Admiralty been only half awake, the delay caused by the faulty propeller would have given time to stop her going to Australia. But the Admiralty—and the War Office—were still in as poor shape as when Brunel embarked on the *Rattler* experiment. When the war began—and after it ended, too—government departments bid against one another for transport with shipowners. The shipowners naturally made the most of their chance and at the beginning of the war a great many steamers were laid down in building yards on the prospect of being chartered at 65s. per gross ton per month. So many sailing ships came forward, however, that this building boom misfired.

For the first job as a troopship the *Great Britain* was sent to Cork where she embarked 38 officers, 31 sergeants, 14 drummer boys, 870 men, two women and three children for Malta where

they arrived on 23 March—a ten-day voyage. She returned to
Portsmouth and from there sailed on 12 April, again for Malta.
The next voyage was again from Cork, this time for the Crimea,
or as the records say, with antiquarian conceit, 'the seat of war'.
She went there only once and took 22 officers, three sergeants,
506 men and 13 women. From Liverpool, calling again at Cork,
she left in February 1856 with 28 officers, 16 sergeants, 692 men
and eight drummer boys for Malta. Five years after the war
it was being claimed that the *Great Britain*, in the 12 months
she was chartered for trooping, had visited ten ports, mostly
in the Mediterranean, and carried 44,000 troops. There are gaps
in the above account, but even if she brought home as many
as she took out—2,500 men—and carried in the interval twice
that number of French troops from Marseilles, the total seems
high. But she may have been used for some intensive short-haul
ferry work. Only once does the *Great Britain* receive a mention
while at the seat of war in a dispatch which shows that war had
not yet been allowed to interfere with the proper exercise of a
gentleman's prose style—the writer was, however, the Navy's
most successful Crimean commander.

'Rear Admiral Sir Edmund Lyons to General Simpson, *Royal
Albert*, off Sebastopol, 1 October 1855. Sir, I have the honour
to inform your Excellency in reply to your letter of today's date
that immediate steps will be taken for the commencement of
the removal of 10,000 Turkish troops from Balaclava to Batoum
and it is desirable that Colonel Simmons should place himself
in immediate communication with Admiral Freemantle when
he will find that the *Great Britain* and other ships have recently
been selected for the service in question. But the completion
of the operation will much depend upon Vivian's contingent
being conveyed to their destination in order that the transports
which have been waiting in the Bosphorous for them for some
time may be at my disposal.'

With a fat Government cheque in the bank, at the war's end
Gibbs, Bright and Co was able to give the *Great Britain* a major
refit. Soon after acquiring the ship the firm, feeling, perhaps, the
need for a title with more flourish, started the process of becoming incorporated as the Liverpool and Australian Navigation
Company under royal charter. This was completed a couple
of years later and the *Great Britain* formally changed owners;
it was only a matter of a different name on advertisements and

letter heads. But the way in which the new name came about left an idea in somebody's mind. Shortly after this name-change —on 24 July 1854—the company took over the beginnings of another iron ship from a bankrupt builder on the river Dee, round the corner from Liverpool. Paterson was invited to design and finish the job which was completed with the launch in August 1855 of—the *Royal Charter*. She ran as a sister ship to the *Great Britain* and was faster under steam (18 knots) and sail (14½ knots) than her sister ship. The *Royal Charter* had a disastrous end. On a return voyage from Australia the passengers said that they wanted to see the *Great Eastern*, then in Holyhead. The captain skirted the Anglesey coast too closely, was caught in a bad storm and the ship was smashed against the rocky shore with a loss of more than 400 lives on 26 October 1859.

From the 1856 refit, which took about nine months, the *Great Britain* emerged with three new masts. These were made by binding four tree trunks together with iron hoops producing very powerful structures capable of delivering more power to drive the old hull along against fast new competition. On 6 August the ship went into the Sandon graving dock where she was fitted up with new and very heavy stern posts and in addition she was equipped with the power to lift the propeller clear of the water altogether. When she first went to sea Brunel and Guppy provided for uncoupling the propeller—this meant in those days unscrewing four bolts and pulling back a connecting unit. It was thought this would take fifteen minutes and reduce drag by 15 per cent. There is no record of the facility being used, although Captain Hosken may have done so on the second transatlantic return voyage when he turned the shattered screw round to the point of least resistance.

There was an element of this early system in the new scheme. A two-ft.-long piece of the propeller shaft—made of wrought iron, 105 ft. long, in four sections, and weighing with its couplings 24 tons—was retractable; it took four men 15 minutes to engage or disconnect this with the propeller. The propeller itself was fixed in a frame shaped like an inverted U; this in turn moved like a sash window inside runners.

With the two-bladed propeller now adopted the hole through which this contrivance was drawn did not need to be very big, providing the propeller blades were in the vertical position.

Although this device incorporated the stern post, and the post on which the rudder hung, it was cumbersome and weighed in all 30 tons and stuck up two feet above the poop deck.

A memory of the contrivance was recalled in 1936 by William Routledge: 'In the waist was a great capstan. Its bar when shipped swept almost the whole breadth of the deck. On the wind gradually strengthening until her canvas alone gave her nine knots all the crew, and the passengers of all classes, manned the bars and with a fiddler on the capstan head, walked the screw up to a rousing chanty to the chorus: "Hurrah, hurrah, for we'll, all, get, blind, drunk, when Johnny comes marching home". The swelling canvas, the straining gear, the vessel's rhythmic sway, the tramp and enthusiasm of the men at the bars, the lilt of the chanty, and the crash of its chorus, never failed to infect the whole ship's company with contagious good humour. She was well manned and handled.'

Apart from the undoubted social advantages for passengers and crew in hauling up the screw this seems a lot of fuss for very little. The first aim was to reduce the drag of the screw in the water when not being used. If all the statistics could be resurrected it would be interesting to work out whether more effort was required to move the burden of the extra weight caused by this contrivance through the water under sail and steam, and compare it with the energy absorbed under sail alone by letting the propeller idle; or by holding it fixed, if two-bladed, in line with the stern post. There was a bonus with the retractable screw—it could be examined and repaired at sea. During this refit, when the *Great Britain* is said to have swarmed with workmen in every part of her from August 1856 to January 1857, the two parallel funnels vanished, being replaced by the final pimple-sized fitting, and the jib boom was strengthened and more steeply angled. This spoiled the smooth bow lines drawn by Paterson.

Another aspect of the refit was changing the passenger arrangements and reducing the total number to be carried. From 1857 there were to be four classes: first, second, third, and steerage. They were designed to hold respectively 78 adults, 19 children, and two infants; 57, eight and five; 117, 23 and six; and 186, 31, and ten. Adding to the space available was a new poop deck. Thus refurbished throughout, the *Great Britain* came out of the graving dock on 24 January 1857 and left for Melbourne on 16

February; she was back in the Mersey on 22 August from her fourth round trip to Australia.

Early in 1857 the Indian Mutiny broke out as both Hindus and Mohammedans rebelled against the arbitrary imposition of European ways, taking their cue from reported reverses in the Crimea, and the depletion of British garrisons on that account. The *Great Britain* was hired on a contract stipulating a 70-day voyage to Bombay to carry relief forces. She went to Cork and on 8 October embarked the 8th Kings Royal Irish Hussars, the 17th Lancers, and a contingent from the 56th Regiment. Among the party was that non-conforming Victorian woman, Mrs Fanny Duberly. She was the wife of a serving officer who had made a name for herself by going to the Crimea and publishing her impressions. The voyage in the *Great Britain* forms a prelude to her second book of military memoirs, *Campaigning experiences in Rajpootana and Central India during the Suppression of the Mutiny.*

They set out into a gale 'which sent us all to our cabins'. But soon 'the sea became tranquil and the manifold beauties of tropical days and nights gradually unfolded themselves—days all gold and nights all silver. Our ship spread her white wings and sailed slowly and gracefully over the foam flecked sparkling waves. Each cavalry regiment had brought its band, refreshed with new instruments since their return from the Crimea, and from 2.30 until 4 p.m. their music completed the luxury of the day.' She soon got bored of this idyll ... 'life on board ship becomes so listless ...' and was glad to see the Cape Verde islands.

There on the quay superintending the 2½ days coaling was the British consul, shabby for such eminence 'and judging from his appearance he is contented with the station in which providence has placed him'. In the harbour there was a Sardinian freighter from South America with 'one of the Princes Buonaparte' on board dying of consumption. The eight army doctors on board the *Great Britain* agreed with the sick man that he would be better off ashore and, against the Sardinian captain's wish, handed the prince over to the consul. 'The relief was, however, too late for next morning as we left the harbour, the consular flag was floating at half mast.

'Captain Gray searched for winds but found none. He was a follower of M. F. Maurey, of the US Navy Dept, whose *Physical*

Geography of the Sea was one of the first books to subject the sea, winds, and currents to scientific treatment. By getting well over to South America and swinging far south of the Cape of Good Hope Maurey calculated in 1853 that he could cut the sailing time to Australia for sailing ships by a quarter (which he gave as 48 days). This theory was not effective on the run to Bombay and a stop had to be made in Table Bay for more coal. For curio collectors there was the sight of the *Great Britain* at anchor with W. S. Lindsay's new 974 gross ton steamer *Ireland*. More interesting to sailors was the sight of the *Great Britain* for the first time alongside the *Himalaya,* the P & O's vast 2,000 horsepower steamer, too big for any trade that could be found in the early 1850s, which was sold to the Government for trooping for £133,000. Fanny Duberly's impression was that 'owing to the tremendous spars and heavy rigging of the *Great Britain* she, although in reality some few feet shorter, appeared the larger of the two'.

Leaving Capetown the weather was bad but it cleared in the Indian Ocean and Mrs Duberly introduces the next captain of the *Great Britain*: 'Mr Chapman our chief mate who had been attacked by sickness, and whose absence was regretted both as an amusing companion and as an admirable seaman, now resumed his place on the deck to the special delectation of Toby, a little spaniel which had come aboard with the 17th Lancers.' The winds were perverse, Mrs Duberly was driven to needlework, and Captain Gray grew very anxious about getting to Bombay by 17 December to catch the outgoing mail steamer with news of his arrival.

'On Tuesday evening, after we had abandoned all expectation of reaching Bombay on the Thursday the wind dropped and the sea grew calm. Every furnace (18 I believe) was alight; the ship throbbed from stem to stern like an overdriven horse; her waste pipes gasped and sobbed and every yard was braced up to offer least resistance to the air. After dinner the health of Captain Gray was given with many just expressions of regard, and the cheers from the saloon were taken up by the men on deck. The ship still strained and panted forward, making such good way during the night that at breakfast the next morning we were greeted with the cheerful news "We shall drop anchor in Bombay harbour this afternoon at 4 o'clock, completing our voyage in 70 days from England, 64 under steam".'

Back in Liverpool, well recompensed for the strain put on her boilers, the *Great Britain*'s owners went through another period of indecision about her best station. She arrived back in the Mersey from Bombay on 10 April. It was not until 28 July that she left—for New York. She spent that winter—out 21 November, back 2 May 1859—on the Australian run, and returned for the last time on 1 July to the transatlantic route. The most probable explanation of this dithery behaviour is that 1857 and 1858 were bad years for British shipping with surplus tonnage looking for work. The repeal of the Navigation Acts attracted blame for this which might more justly have been placed on Crimean War speculation.

From this point the *Great Britain* stayed continuously on the Australian run until 1876, making over the 15 years a total of 27 voyages—by itself a considerable record. Her career settles into an uneventful routine—matching that of the country after which she was named, then approaching the height of its dominance with, as Gladstone said in 1865, an 'intoxicating augmentation of wealth and power'. No such infusion swelled the profit column in the *Great Britain*'s account. In her GWSSCo days her success was always 'scientifically speaking'. Now under the Liverpool and Australian Navigation Company she enjoyed a reputation as 'a universally popular ship', and 'a household word'. But although undoubtedly the most successful auxiliary steamer she seems not to have been profitable. Gibbs, Bright's records have been destroyed, and the official history (of Antony Gibbs Sons & Co) says only that the *Great Britain* was 'very popular with the passengers, though the operating results were disappointing'.

Why the *Great Britain* did not make a comfortable profit must have puzzled her owners. She was the best answer to the mid-century problem of getting quickly to the other end of the earth, which was beyond the range of pure steamers. Using her advantages she made consistently good times—55 days 17 hours was her best but the roll call is presented: 56, 58, 62, 63, 59, 60, 58, 61, and four 57s, for a dozen outbound voyages in the 1860s.

No Gibbs, Bright balance sheets have come to light. It is hard, therefore, to discover what is meant by 'disappointing'. It can hardly mean that the ship made a continuous substantial loss, otherwise she would not have been kept on the line. It is true that the company leadership became deeply affected by John

Henry Newman's Oxford Movement—to the extent that departments in the firm became known internally as 'sadducees',
'epiphany', and so on, while the senior partner was referred to
as 'prior'. But this influence did not in any other way lead the
company to operate as a charity, and there is little reason to
think that the *Great Britain* was an exception. It is tempting
to assume that the lost space to cargo due to the engine room—
rather more than a third of the tonnage measured volumetrically
(1,464 tons)—and the 20-odd men employed to work the engines
absorbed the profits. These factors must have played a part. But
wage levels were low and static. The total wage bill for a five-
month round trip only came to £3,000; say she used 700 tons of
coal out and home—£1,050; on the first Australian voyage,
worked out against a 60-days duration expectancy, the victual-
ling costs were over 3s. a head for passengers and crew; assuming
this remained the provision rate the bill for a round trip was
about £13,000. In all, a total of around £17,000 spread over five
months. With a 75 per cent load factor out and home, the receipts amounted to over £20,000. All we know about what the
Great Britain carried is what the *Great Britain* newspaper tells
us—'she has been most successful on each occasion in getting
her full complement of passengers'.

Only towards the end of the *Great Britain*'s career does any
reflection of the accountants' anxieties appear in the ship's
papers. In the Agreement and Account of Crew for the voyage
starting 22 September 1873 a note says: 'Seamen and firemen
mutually to assist one another.' A feature, incidentally, which
the framers of a new Merchant Seaman's Act in 1971 are seeking to include.

'Uneventful' used to describe the later history of a ship like
the *Great Britain* leaves plenty of room for run-of-the-mill
troubles. Gladys Robinson of Yeronga, Brisbane, has a long
letter written by her father in 1909 correcting errors in a local
magazine about the *Great Britain*. Arthur Robinson was well
placed to make corrections—as a native of West Derby, Liverpool, he had watched as an 11-year-old boy the *Great Britain*
being towed back up the Mersey from Dundrum. He travelled
out to Australia in her, leaving Liverpool in November 1858.

He recalled: 'We were bowling along before the wind with
every available stitch of canvas and studding sail booms out-
rigged when, just before break of day, we ran into an American

barque. She struck us on the port bow, grinding along right to amidships, and tearing away our rigging. When I got on deck it looked like a mass of tangle overhead—every yard on the foremast except the royal was broken and hanging in all directions, and the main and topsail yards on the main mast were badly damaged. Seeing a group of sailors forward I ran along and they were just hauling up a sailor who had been lowered over the bows to see what damage was done to our hull. He was just telling, in sailors language, that there was a big bulge but no hole—adding that if we had struck a little harder we could all have been in Davy Jones's locker by this time. I could plainly see the barque. Her foremast had broken off about the middle and had fallen back on the main mast.

'As soon as we found we were in no immediate danger a boat was lowered and the mate put off to the Yankee to see if he wanted any assistance, but he would not accept any help, and, according to the mate's account, was very abusive and said he would not get out of the way of any damned steamer afloat.' Which must have reinforced the American legend in the *Great Britain*'s forecastle.

Much the same kind of incident happened shortly after midnight on 21 September 1861 just off Cape Otway on the approaches to Melbourne. A ship was seen going the opposite way about two points on the port bow. 'I at once put the helm to port,' reported chief officer Charles Turner, 'and to my astonishment discerned that he put his helm to starboard by his red light becoming obscure. Seeing a collision was evident I at once ordered the engines to be stopped which was complied with. My helm being hard to port at the same time the starboard bow of the steamer came into violent contact with my port bow carrying away my jib guys, bail ropes, cut water, and figurehead; then falling alongside, stove in the port bridge boat.' Captain Gray asked if the other ship was in danger and got the answer 'I cannot say'. It steamed away and further hails were not answered. The *Great Britain* was found to be 'in perfect safety' and went on to Melbourne.

On a smaller scale, the official logs detail more domestic tragedies. On 10 August 1861 at 10 a.m., for instance, 'John Merrick, carpenter, lost finger (little) of right hand caught underneath the hause hole door while shutting it'. Ten days before 'Richard Howard, gold digger, died from an apoplectic seizure in a moment, Thos. Morland, surgeon'.

It is clear from the logs that Captain Gray operated a mild Shetland Islands freemasonry when it came to hiring men; in 1862 he had Robert Peterson as first mate, and Gilbert Peterson as second mate. Two years later John Angus joins as fourth mate. In between Peter Christie was third mate. These could be put down to natural statistical causes, perhaps, as the Shetland Islanders were notable seamen. But how to explain the little Shetland colony in the quartermaster's store in 1863 when all four inhabitants—John Sinclair, Thomas Scott, William Slater, and Gilbert Johnson were Shetlanders?

The *Great Britain*'s 'hard case' was James Parry, aged 20, who on 18 October 1870 'assaulted James Battersby, steward, with closed hands producing swelling and blackness around each eye whereby he forfeits two days' pay'. Three years later, on 30 June 1873, Parry offended on a grander scale, earning the entry 'James Parry, assistant steward, was drunk and riotous assaulting the master, mate, and purser, using most profane and obscene language to his superior officers thereby necessitating the master to have said James Parry manacled for the safety of all; while securing the said James Parry he wilfully damaged the purser's watch and chain to the extent of £5 which the said James Parry agrees to pay, the same to be deducted from his wages'. Ironically, one of James Parry's discharge certificates marked 'VG' for very good behaviour survives among the papers.

The voyage starting on 17 March 1870 was notable for a much less straightforward and more serious upset. The log book gives the bare bones of the drama that must have taken place. On 6 April Richard Hulse, fourth engineer, was disrated for drunkenness. He was absent from duty when the ship got to Australia for three days, and on 25 May was unfit through drink for 24 hours. On 21 May, Alexander Meadon, the chief engineer, was 'discharged by mutual consent'. Two firemen deserted on 17 May and two more on the 23rd. Both Meadon and Hulse had been with the ship for at least ten years, and although desertions and mutual discharges were quite common the engine room seems hitherto to have been a contented place. To add to the captain's troubles Thomas Christie, then second officer, discharged himself, followed by the surgeon, Alfred Puddicombe.

Otherwise the *Great Britain* emerges as a happy ship. There were deaths on board through accident and illness—and this entry: 'Robert Lawson, 1st class passenger, committed suicide by jumping overboard 4 April 1869.' There were at least as many births, and being born on board often meant being marked for life. The mother of a former mayoress of Hastings was born off Cape Horn on 17 February 1867 and given the Christian names Maud Gray. More unusual was John Great Britain Donaldson who was born on another homeward trip and later gave song recitals, accompanied by his niece, in Liberal clubs in Lancashire. Commenting that his name probably made it easier to get engagements, the niece, Mrs B. Wilkinson of Preston, wrote: 'The clubs in those days were not like the ones of today.... He was a lovely tenor singer and always sang *nice* songs wherever he went or my parents would not have let me go to play for him.'

The oddest log book entry says that on 9 June 1864 at 3 p.m. James Aikin, assistant steward did the deed which led to his being 'herewith charged with throwing overboard two beds the property of passengers in a wilful manner; he must under the circumstances on arrival in Melbourne or other port or ports reimburse the said passengers with new beds or pay the equivalent value thereof'.

Feuds like the one that produced that incident form no part, of course, of the *Great Britain*'s vehicle for literary invention— the ship's newspaper. First with the piano, the ship must also have been very early in the field with a printing press on board. The papers had at least three titles, *The Great Britain Times*, *The Cabinet*, and *The Great Britain Gazette*. These were printed on board. *The Great Britain Magazine*, or *Weekly Screw* was printed in Melbourne. These journals gave the editors a chance to poke highly stylised fun at fellow passengers, and give records of the vessel's weekly progress. They show signs of strain, especially in the jokes section where the offerings scar the memory: 'Why do you think the Line was broken before we crossed it? Because the *Great Britain* was obliged to *knot* it.' 'Why is the noble commander of the *Great Britain* expected to be always prepared to risk his life for his Queen and country? Because he is one of the *Scots Greys*.' 'In what respect do the saloon passengers disapprove of Captain Gray's navigation? While he keeps to one course as long as he can, they expect four courses within a single hour.' It is almost a relief to turn to: 'My Native Land.

O Scotia! dearest, happiest land!' Abundant space was provided for poems about home.

In the official log there is great detail about minor disciplinary offences. But the really big event in the long years that the *Great Britain* spent going to and from Australia receives the tersest of entries. 'Tuesday 26 November 1872 Latitude 31° 30′ S: Longitude 21° 12′ West. 7 a.m. Captain Gray not to be found. Supposed to have committed suicide by going through one of the stern ports, it having been shut by John Prout, steward, at 10 p.m. on the 25th inst, and afterwards found open with lanyard let go and crossbar removed on the morning of the 26th inst. Signed Peter Robertson, chief officer, Austin Unsworth, Purser, William S. Smythe, Surgeon.' Captain Gray's belongings were then listed—as the regulations required. There may have been an official inquiry, but if so its findings are not preserved among Board of Trade records. The only surviving amplification is in the Liverpool papers.

This is what the *Liverpool Courier* said on 27 December. 'The voyage of the *Great Britain* just completed after a run of 62 days has been marked by an exceedingly melancholy circumstance in the death of Captain John Gray, Lieutenant RNR, so long and so favourably known in connection with the celebrated liner which he has commanded for nearly 20 years. Captain Gray's sad end is shrouded in mystery. On the evening of the 24 November about 11 when the vessel had passed Cape Horn about two days, the Captain retired to his cabin. About five o'clock next morning his cabin boy entered and found the apartment unoccupied, but thinking that the Captain was probably on deck, the boy took no notice of the circumstance for some time. As soon as he communicated the fact to the vessel's officers, they made every search, but the Captain could nowhere be found.

'Upon an examination of the cabin where he slept it appeared that the "stern window" was open, and the conclusion is that the unfortunate gentleman, whether in a state of somnolency or not will never be ascertained, had fallen or jumped through the window. Deceased had been in conversation with several of his officers shortly before retiring to rest on the previous evening, and nothing unusual was observed in his manner; nor has anything transpired to throw light on the mysterious circumstances of his death. Captain Gray had been most if not the whole of his life in the service of Messrs Gibbs, Bright owners of the *Great Britain*, having been for some time first officer of that steamship under Captain B. R. Mathews.

'He was appointed to command the vessel early in the year 1854 and in that position gained a high reputation for his abilities as a seaman and his courteous and gentlemanly conduct towards all with whom his official duties brought him into contact. The deceased, who resided in Upper Parliament Street, and was 52, leaves a widow and four children lamenting his loss. He had long contemplated retiring from the sea and it was understood that this was to have been his last voyage had all been well. The inexpressibly sad nature of the occurrence was heightened by the fact that Mrs Gray accompanied by her daughters went down to the Princes Stage on Christmas day to meet the Captain only however to learn of his melancholy end.'

The *Liverpool Post* felt confident enough to headline its account 'Suicide of Captain Gray of the *Great Britain*'—and said 'he suddenly threw himself overboard and was drowned'. The *Journal of Commerce* added 'so far as can be ascertained at present, it appears that Captain Gray had been in ill-health for some days previous to his disappearance'. In the Shetlands there is still a suspicion—lacking solid foundation—that he was murdered by a steward who knew him to be secretly carrying home a large quantity of gold in his cabin. The first officer, Mr Peter Robertson, brought the *Great Britain* home.

Peter Robertson reverted from the rank of acting-captain to chief officer on the appointment of Charles Henry Chapman, aged 49, born in Lincoln, living at 68 Wellington Street, Liverpool, to be master of the *Great Britain*. He had made at least three voyages in the ship as mate (or chief officer), and had more recently been in command of the Liverpool and Australian Navigation Company's sailing ship *Alsager*. He made three round trips as master, and a memento of this period survives— a heavy gold ring inscribed 'Chapman from Johnson' which has an internal diameter of 9/10ths of an inch. In the winter of 1874 Captain Chapman was going down the Pier Head in Liverpool to visit the ship when he fell from the horse tram, developed Bright's disease, and died on 21 June. He signed in the shakiest of hands the crew agreement for the voyage which began on 11 January 1875; but his name is crossed out with the comment 'Sick—did not join the ship'.

Everybody moved up one, and Peter Robertson, aged 37, from Leith but now living in Liverpool, took over for the second time the captaincy of the *Great Britain*. He was the last holder of the position under the L & ANC. He commanded the ship on two round trips, the first starting in 11 January, the second on 6 July 1875. This last voyage was unique in being scheduled 'Liverpool to Melbourne, via London'. Her strange presence in the Thames provided the best known photograph of the *Great Britain* as she looked in her Australian hey-day.

There is a valediction to those days. 'It was 5 a.m. on a bright summer's morning in the 1870s in the good ship *Theophane*, a well-known Liverpool clipper,' wrote a contributor to *Sea Breezes* in 1920, 'when the writer, a boy, reported a sail on the port bow to the 2nd officer. He took the telescope and after a good look turned to the boy and said, "Nick, its the old *Great Britain*". Shortly afterwards the captain, a well-known Liverpool shipmaster Thomas Follit, appeared and the 2nd officer reported the ship in sight and what he thought she was. "The devil it is; if so we'll show her our heels." At noon we were abeam, and noticed the *Great Britain* was steaming as well as sailing, and they set their top-mast and lower stunsails. Our stunsail booms had been sent down and the stunsails stowed away a few days before. At 8 p.m. the *Great Britain* was out of sight astern. The next day we saw nothing of each other, but on the day after when running up the Irish coast we saw the *Great Britain*'s royals and topgallant sails astern about 4 p.m. At 8 p.m. we lost them astern again. The first watch that night we were running about 13½ knots with the yards just off the backstays and leerail under. Next morning with a light air off Holyhead the *Great Britain* passed us all sail furled and under steam. When abeam her passengers crowded on the rail and rigging and boats and gave us a real good cheer. The good old ship got into the Mersey on tide, before us, and thus ended her wonderful career as a Melbourne passenger auxiliary steamer, this being her last voyage in that trade.'

Nobody knew until it was over that the *Great Britain* had made her last trip to Australia. She would have been given a memorable send-off from Melbourne. But if she had to go, 1876 was a good year to choose. For in that year for the first time the number of steamships launched outnumbered the sailing ships. Alfred Holt had developed the compound engine—one that used the same steam twice at different stages of expansion—so that it was efficient enough to carry 3,000 tons of cargo and enough coal to steam at ten knots for 9,000 miles non-stop. Twin-screw ships had come in on the Atlantic and in the late 1860s the Inman Line's *City of Paris* won the Blue Riband with a speed of over 20 knots. Holt's steamers went to Foochow in 65 days, so that the *Great Britain*, with her 60 days plus to Melbourne, was still just about competitive in speed. But inevitably, the *Great Britain*'s age began to tell. Compared with the technically more advanced ships her costs grew. Edward Grace complained of 'the thump, thump of the screw'; cold stores replaced the floating farmyard of livestock carried to supply fresh meat. And by 1876 it must have been matter for amused comment to see one's friends off to Australia in a vessel still painted up with mock Nelsonian gun ports.

No more is heard of the ship until 29 July 1881 when the *Liverpool Mercury* said: 'This vessel, which has a history of more than ordinary interest, was yesterday offered for sale by Mr C. W. Kellock (Messrs Kellock & Co) at their salesroom Walmer Buildings, Water Street, and the event attracted a very large attendance of gentlemen who are closely identified with the shipping interests of the port. The *Great Britain* lying in the West Float, Birkenhead, was described in the bill of particulars as of 3,270 gross tonnage and 1,795 tons net register. It is further stated that "she was for many years in the Australia trade and well known by her rapid passages as a most successful ship". Her construction is of great strength and the iron used was of the finest quality. For the cattle trade across the Atlantic she is admirably adapted, her high tween decks and side ports affording grand ventilation and she can carry livestock on three decks. For a sailing ship her beautiful lines peculiarly adapt her, and with machinery taken out she is calculated to carry 4,000 tons deadweight. Her engines are by J. Penn and Sons of Greenwich, and are in good condition; her boilers are by Fawcett Preston & Co of Liverpool; and though this steamer has been built many years her iron was so good and the strength of construction so great, that with a certain outlay she could be made a most desirable merchant ship. The bidding began at £2,000, then went to £5,000, and before long £6,500 was offered. There being no advance on this price Mr Kellock announced that the vessel was withdrawn.'

Six months later the *Great Britain* was sold—on 19 January 1882—to James Charles Hayne of 15 Bishopgate Street, London. Antony Gibbs' London office was in Bishopgate St, and Hayne was probably proposed by the company as nominal owner. On 2 November 1882 the ownership changed to Vicary Gibbs, bringing the ship back in name as well as fact within the original 'family' of Bristol businessmen. The Honourable Vicary Gibbs was the second son in the generation of the Gibbs family which consolidated all the company's British ramifications into Antony Gibbs, Sons, & Co. He was a grandson of George Henry Gibbs, GWR promoter. Whether he resumed the connection with the *Great Britain* because it was a bargain or an heirloom is not known; neither is the price he paid.

By this time Antony Gibbs' business was heavily concentrated on South America and revolved around shipping guano —sea-bird manure—from Peru. From this the company extended into other bulk cargoes like timber, nitrates, and coal. The *Great Britain* was to join this bulk cargo fleet. Her engines were taken out and she was sheathed in $3\frac{1}{2}$-in.-thick pitch pine from a point nine feet above her keel to slightly more than 25 feet above the keel—a great wooden corset, 16 feet from top to bottom, clapped on to the old body with 7/8th-in. galvanised iron bolts. On top of this was thin zinc plating over a felt base. H & C Grayson, the firm which did the work, has vanished into the Cammell Laird empire, taking with it the price asked for the job, and more importantly the reason for it.

No conclusive answer about the wooden cladding of the *Great Britain* has been given. There have been lots of suggestions: the wood was to insulate the ship in the tropics; it was to protect her from exuberant pilotage by lightermen in South American ports; or to check wind-and-water fouling along the water line. But by this date progress was being made with anti-fouling paints; and if this was the reason why was the ship not completely sheathed underwater? In the Royal Navy wood cladding was used for HMS *Inconstant* in 1866, and almost to the end of the century, to protect iron hulls from looking 'like a lawyer's wig'. The wooden outer covering prevented electrolytic corrosion which always occurred when copper or zinc were put directly over iron.

There were particular reasons in the *Great Britain*'s case that may have contributed to the decision to sheathe her in wood.

She was the first big iron ship; no one knew how long an iron ship *could* last. She was to be more heavily laden in her new part than before and the wood could have been put on to strengthen her; Lloyds refused to classify her in 1872, but gave her an 'A1' rating (its highest) ten years later—perhaps because she was stronger. The reasons must have been powerful because it is said that the cladding cost as much as a new ship. While it was being done, the modest superstructure which the *Great Britain* had acquired over the years was swept away, the lifeboats reduced to four; but the basic 1857 profile remained with the great masts, and the high-kicking jib boom. The *Great Britain* was now registered at 2,735 gross tons, 2,640 net tons.

For her first voyage it was decided to send the *Great Britain* round the Horn to San Francisco with coal, and have her fetch back cheap grain for Ireland from the prairies. Confusion reigned over signing the crew. James Morris, aged 38, signed on as master on 11 November 1882 with a crew of 42. He was discharged on 28 November. On the following day F. Kerr signed on as master, was discharged, and signed on again as mate. He was not a happy choice—better perhaps as mate than master for when he left in San Francisco the comment next to his name was 'drunkenness and neglect of duty'. Henry Stap, aged 53, was the captain finally selected.

The voyage was a disaster. The *Great Britain* sailed at the end of November, and almost at once put back to Liverpool leaking. She was surveyed and sailed again on 2 December. The crew complement was captain, mate, carpenter, boatswain, steward, cook, 28 seamen, and four apprentices. It seems as if only 17 able seamen signed the agreement and two of these did not join. Those who joined hated it. On 12 December William Jones fell overboard from the main rigging and drowned, his effects being sold off among the rest of the crew to recoup for the ship his advance of wages. When she reached Montevideo the crew refused to go on unless she was lightened; she was surveyed again and 500 tons were taken from her lower hold and stored between decks to ease her. Twelve of the crew deserted. Captain Stap recruited 11 new men at £3. 10s. a month (£2. 15s. in England); then he went 70 miles up the River Plate to Buenos Aires and found another ten men at £4 a month. Then he picked up another six in Montevideo. With this assortment the *Great Britain* arrived in San Francisco in June.

They all vanished in San Francisco. Twenty-seven fresh seamen signed on at £5 on 29 August, and the ship's new mate was
John Ramsey, a Canadian. This crew held together, with the
exception of Patrick Lowe, a stowaway who left in Montevideo,
until she docked in Liverpool on 9 February 1884. The next
voyage was quieter; perhaps the clue is that there are 44 names
on the crew list. Twenty-nine left, mostly deserted, in San
Francisco but Captain Stap was able to collect another 20 including a large contingent of Norwegians. This trip ended in Liverpool on 16 July 1885.

Before what was to be the last voyage the Bristol connection
was at last severed and the *Great Britain* sailed under the
managing ownership of R. W. Leyland of Exchange Buildings,
Liverpool. This company existed from 1882 to 1894 as owners of
a fleet of large sailing ships called after districts in and near
Liverpool. Its latest acquisition sailed from Cardiff for Panama
on 6 February 1886. There could be no arguments about loading
because the 'Plimsoll line' had now reached the *Great Britain*.
'The position of the load line disc which now indicates the
summer freeboard shall not be altered,' said a handwritten note
in the crew agreement. Thirty-five hands were stipulated as a
complete crew, but 37 signed. These men spent six weeks pushing slowly—her rough log showed that she never went above
seven knots—towards Cape Horn; there is a suggestion that her
cargo had caught fire by that stage. A savage squall hit the ship
from the south-west and smashed her fore and main topmasts.
The crew fought for ten hours to clear the wreckage as the vessel
wallowed on the very edge of destruction. When the prospect of
saving her appeared the crew insisted that Captain Stap turn
back—which he did not want to do. But the broken masts, the
saturated state of the crew's quarters, the lack of fresh water as
the sea had broached the storage tanks, argued the men's case
forcefully. The ship hobbled back to the Falklands.

Avoiding the Falklands was almost as powerful an argument
in favour of continuing the voyage as the crew was able to muster
for going back. Run by the Falkland Island Company, Port
Stanley, the capital, collected ships from the South Atlantic as a
spider collects flies. Basil Lubbock wrote: 'Port Stanley has
always been dreaded by shipmasters being notorious for its
heavy charges and leisurely ways of work which has to be put
up with by the lame ducks. Even as far back as 1887 ship's

carpenters in the Falklands were receiving 16s. 9d. a day and blacksmith's 20s. while 3s. an hour was being paid overtime.' This compares with 55s. a month for a seaman.

With winter closing in, the *Great Britain* dragged herself towards Port Stanley. She went aground at the entrance in thick weather, but soon came off without damage. Two days later she again touched the same bank getting under way to be towed to Stanley. She arrived there on 24 May 1886 unwillingly, and almost certainly unnecessarily, at the end of her sailing career. Every voice that spoke about the ship from Port Stanley was the voice of the Falkland Island Co. The first cable out (via Montevideo) said 'The *Great Britain*, Stap, from Cardiff for Panama which put in here in distress has lost fore and main topmasts and sustained much damage to rigging; her hull is a good deal strained and her cargo shifted and damaged by seawater.... The surveyor's report states that repairs will amount to £5,500. Considering that water has got down among the coal it is desirable that the cargo should be forwarded as soon as possible. The master awaits instructions from England before doing anything.'

A repeat of this telegram was sent out ten days later, and yet another—'she is seriously strained and is leaking'—was wired on 15 June. The independent opinion reached Liverpool on 16 July and was published in the *Shipping Gazette* on 23 July: 'The Liverpool Salvage Association's special officer cables from Montevideo last evening—"*Great Britain* survey held, surveyor's reporting ship quite tight."' But this was almost too late for any action to be taken; the crew started trickling away on 24 June, until by the 4 October they had all gone. They went away on other ships; of the few that stayed Charlie Enestrom, then 21, remained for many years the best known *Great Britain* survivor in the Falklands.

E. Rathenham Brully, Shipping Master in the Falklands, drew the final line under the *Great Britain*'s active life on 30 November 1886. 'I hereby certify that the remainder of the crew of the within described vessel have been duly paid off, and those electing to proceed to England have been duly sent home. I further certify that the *Great Britain* has been sold at this port to the Falkland Islands Company of 39 Gracechurch Street, London EC.'

Making a living in the South Atlantic is tough and the Falkland Island Co had to drive hard bargains to survive. It had complete control over prices charged for repair work, and some influence over the giving of seaworthiness certificates. If the company took a fancy to a damaged ship for use as a floating warehouse for company produce, that ship's owners had to fight hard and pay dearly to get their vessel out.

Captain A. B. Garwood, who lived his last years in Arundel, Sussex, has left a note about the *Great Britain*. 'The Falkland Island Company made an offer for the ship and cargo which was rejected; because of this the sharks condemned the ship and refused to allow her to leave. In the end they got ship and cargo (4,500 tons of coal) very cheaply. The ship I was in then, HMS *Swallow*, coaled from her and I found the old scrap log for that voyage—she never showed more than seven knots per hour. The last I saw of the *Great Britain* in 1889 was as a store ship, all the coal had been discharged and large doors fitted in her lower decks where the island produce of wool, hides, and tallow was stored from the coasters to await the then monthly call of steamers bound from the West Coast of South America—the German Kosmos Line.'

From here Mr A. G. Nelson Jones, Port Stanley Harbour Master, takes up the end of the story in 1934. He says in a letter to Liverpool Museum that the *Great Britain*'s cargo was only 3,200 tons of coal, but confirms that the Admiralty considered, but rejected, the idea of using the ship as a coaling station for the South American Squadron. The spars and masts were cut in 1887. 'Since the year 1929 the hulk has been empty and moored in Stanley Harbour. It is unlikely that she will be broken up, but quite probably grounded in one of the bays in the near vicinity.' Captain Stap, the most elusive of the *Great Britain*'s masters, went on to command Leyland's *Halewood*, and *Ditton*, a mighty 2,901 tons gross ship launched in 1891 when he was 62, His former charge was then 48, but had a lot of life left in her.

CHAPTER VI

Travellers' Tales

During the years she journeyed to and from Australia the *Great Britain* produced—inspired would be to put it too strongly—a good number of diarists and journal-keepers. Eight or nine weeks' prospective idleness turned the mid-Victorian mind naturally towards devising some useful or improving achievement. With one minor exception the diaries that have come to light so far were written between 1860 and 1872, the period when the *Great Britain* had finished the re-fits, occasional re-runs on the transatlantic ferry, and military contracts.

This concentration of records in the mid '60s and early '70s suggests that long ocean voyages were gradually becoming more commonplace among reflective middle-class people. They were no longer hazardous ventures in which hands were used either for holding on or praying for deliverance. The *Great Britain* was big enough, safe enough, and, yes, boring enough to give her passengers the feeling of being internees rather than hostages; many took the educated captives' way out, and wrote a diary.

The most famous account of life on board the Gibbs, Bright ship is that by Rachel Henning whose *Letters* have achieved fame in Australia. She was the product of English vicarage society and she followed her brother out to Australia, had doubts and came back, and then finally returned in the *Great Britain* in 1861 to Australia where she eventually married and became Mrs Taylor. She etches a polished account of life in the first class saloon. But there were acute, if less mannered, sensibilities in the steerage.

John McLennan is listed in the State Library of Victoria as 'aged 20 years; single, ploughman; Scotch' on arrival in Melbourne on 12 February 1868. He was a 'warrant' passenger—Government assisted—on the voyage from Liverpool that began on 13 December 1867. His youth, small beginnings, and subsidised passage did not inhibit McLennan from addressing from the outset a wider audience than Miss Henning. He starts: 'Dear reader I would have you to understand that their is all sorts of classes Emigrates to the colloney, their is a great many in this ship that payes their passage, but still, any one leaving their own country, and going to another, are emigrants the same as I am also I would have you to know that their is bad behaviour to be got among the better class as well as the poor class although not so much taken notice of. I will try to quote the few remarks which is to the Best of my knowledge Founded upon Facts.'

Portentous for a ploughman in any age, but McLennan changes at once into a more homely style to describe his arrival in Liverpool, 'Dear Friends, it was on the night of the 11th December, that I parted with my Dearest friends, which made me feel sorry beyond expression, one is apt to say I may never see you again. But we must always hope for the better, and trust in God so that everything may be done for our good, I went along in the train till I came to Perth, during that time which I felt very dull, and my mind went wandering back and fore, thinking on things past and things to come, I arrived at Perth early in the morning, and I thought I would wait in Perth, till the through train at night came, so I went Back and fore, through Perth all day and in the evening I met with the Footman that was in Sanquhar house, Forres, when I was their and I had a bottle of beer with him before train time came.

'I thought I would meet with some others going by this train, as it would arrive in Liverpool at 6 o'clock in the morning of the day appointed, so when the train came in I met in with a woman that was going to the *GB* she was in the coloney before, she was going out to her man, we went along till we came to Motherwell station where we changed carriages, and we went into the train that came from Glasgow, their I met with six, who was my companions during the rest of the voyage, we went on to Liverpool, and as it was rather early when we arrived, we went and had a little refreshment, which a young man that was coming in the train with us, was kind enough to pay for us all, after it was daylight, we got a man to take down our boxes down to the boat that crosses to Birkenhead, we paid a shilling each, the ferry boat was only 2d. each, and a cart belonging to the comisioners [the Government Emigration Commissioners] took our luggage to the depot, we went into the depot early thinking we would get out again, but we was very much mistaken, and I had no sheets nor soap, but I could have them inside, only I had to pay more

for them, we was very bad used at the depot, we got bad meat
and we did not get enough of it. They had two dirty looking
Greacy looking cooks.

'We was their till Friday the 13th when a smal [steamer]
came for us about noon, and took us out to the Briton, she was
lying in the mercy, the rest of the Passengers was on board but
they did not come in at the same Place as us, when we was lying
their I could see the *Great Eastern* at a distance the largest ship
in the world she has six masts, next day we hoaled Anchor bore
away down the river.'

Others arrived less wide-eyed. Thomas Atkinson left Euston
on the 10 a.m. express on 10 August 1869, arrived at Lime Street
at 3.10 p.m. and took a cab to the Gibbs, Bright office—the main
one was at 1, North John St. He was on his way back to Australia after a long visit. Boisterous weather had kept the *Great
Britain* in dock, and he went down and stored his boxes in his
cabin 'which was much smaller than I expected'. After dinner
at the Angel Hotel in Dale St he spent the night with friends in
Waterloo, north of Liverpool. Next day, after letter-writing and
shopping, he was at Princes Landing Stage at 5 p.m. to take the
tender out to the *Great Britain*. He saw 'a good many passengers
going off, especially steerage passengers—and tons of luggage'.

Miss Henning noted the 'curious' state of the Black Country
between Dudley and Wolverhampton on her train journey from
Kirby Lonsdale to Liverpool. 'The whole country ploughed up
for miles by mines and covered with furnaces and tall chimneys
and wretched brick houses.' She, too, went to the Angel 'which is
very comfortable and clean. We had tea and poached eggs,
settled accounts, and went to bed. Mr Boyce [her brother-in-law]
said he was hardly at all tired. I was rather.' Boyce went to James
Baines' offices (this was shortly after Baines' Black Ball Line had
merged with Gibbs, Bright's) where he met Captain Gray. 'And
on his mentioning my name to him,' writes Rachel Henning,
'he remembered me perfectly at Melbourne and said he would
call on me, which he did, and very kind it was considering all
he must have to do on the eve of his ship sailing. He is a most
jolly and genial-looking sailor, speaking broad Lancashire.' [Miss
Henning's ear is almost certainly at fault—Captain Gray was
born in the Shetlands and remained there till he was a man.]

Esteem was mutual between the passenger and captain and
Captain Gray later gave Rachel Henning a bracelet which the

family still has. It was the mid-nineteenth century custom for voyagers to give presents to captains and this reversal indicates a degree of rapport. With this happy link established Rachel Henning went down (on 14 February 1861) at three p.m. 'only Mr Boyce and I, took all my luggage on board except the carpet-bags, and saw my cabin. It is a comfortable little place enough, the berths look very much so, and my cabin companion has been so ill advised as to take the upper one, which I am very glad of.

'I heard at Baines' office who my cabin companion was—a Mrs Bronchardt. They said she was a nice lady-like person, but I shall have to find out about that. The last steamer, which is only for the first class passengers, goes off at five o'clock tomorrow evening, I do not suppose Mr Boyce will be allowed to go on board with me as it is against the rules.... I unpacked and put some things in order while Mr Boyce screwed up the little cupboard in a convenient corner and made things look quite comfortable.... The bag of tools is worth its weight in gold. I have driven innumerable nails for Mrs Bronchardt and myself, and though the steward did come and inquire if the carpenter was in our cabin yesterday, as he was particularly wanted, no one has found any fault with the nails, and the cupboard which Mr Boyce screwed up behind the funnel has never been seen and is most useful.... The cabin is so light that I can read well in bed, and the lamp shines into my berth, so, that being the case, I have nailed up a moreen bag just within reach of my hand, and put a little store of books into it; also my lantern matches, camphor, etc.'

If a hammer and nails were a luxury, perhaps a slightly furtively indulged one, in the first class, they were a necessity in steerage—if you knew enough to bring them. William Moly-neux, aged 23, and his wife Betsy, 21, didn't know when they reached the ship on 10 August 1869. They arrived 'about two o'clock after a great deal of trouble with tickets and procuring kit. Berths looked gloomy till one got accustomed to the light. Found out I had nothing proper for hanging kits. Went into the town to procure hooks and also padlock for berth, got wet through.' Next day revealed new deficiencies—'No water to wash or drink, had to find out a place and when found had the satisfaction to find the [mess?] tins run out, changed what I could and dearly wished I had known before leaving Birmingham to have had the proper utensils made.'

William Molyneux, with some breakfast inside him, 'had a turn of the windlass to assist in hauling the ship out of the basin till dinner. Cannot eat the ships biscuits (Bought two loaves about a mouthful 6d. each). After dinner we were towed out of the last basin.' Some shipowners and masters argued that crews should be kept small on emigrant ships because passengers could double up as crew in emergencies. This was not the case on the *Great Britain* but no doubt the travellers were glad to be allowed sometimes to help sail the ship. They were only invited to do so in harmless circumstances.

Rachel Henning set out into conditions that proved far from harmless. 'We sailed as you know on Sunday the 17th, had a quiet night enough, and Monday was tolerably calm till the evening, when it began to blow; and during the night we had such a gale as is seldom met with. It *did* blow with a vengeance. The captain and all the officers were on deck all night; indeed the former has not been in bed since we left Liverpool, such has been the weather. I saw him to speak to in the morning and he said he had never had the *Great Britain* out in such weather before.'

'However there was no great damage done beyond making everyone, nearly, extremely ill and sorely frightened, and the wind went down in the course of the next day. We had very rough weather during Tuesday and Wednesday, but still nothing remarkable, but yesterday morning it began to blow again, and for about six hours we had such a hurricane as no one on board ever saw before. To say that I never knew anything like it is nothing at all, but all the oldest sailors say a West Indian tornado was the only thing it was like.

'Providentially, it came by daylight: began about nine, and the worst was over by three. I could never give you the least idea of the force or roar of the wind, and some of the passengers who ventured on deck said the *Great Britain*, big as she is, looked like a cockleshell among the waves, and that it seemed impossible but that she must be buried among them.

'She behaved admirably, took in very little water, and came up as stiff as possible after every roll. Several seas came on board, however; one broke into the saloon and thence into the cabins, one of which was three feet deep in water. The steward mopped and dipped it out in buckets. Some water got into our cabin and on going in to investigate I found that one of my boxes was standing in a puddle; and remembering that the children's likeness was at the bottom of that very box, I determined gale or no gale to unpack it and get the picture out which I did. It was not in the least hurt.'

The *Great Britain* was damaged and made for Queenstown. 'The foreyard was sprung and a sprit sail hook broken; the bulwarks smashed in in one place and a boat stove in and half knocked away by a wave, and they had to cut her away as she was beating in the ship's side. This boat was a great affliction to me as the name of the ship was on her, but it will be all right now you can hear we are safe.

'They report that one of the masts is sprung, but I cannot make out if it is true. How they ever stood at all I cannot imagine. The captain expected some of them to go, for he had axes laid all ready to cut away the wreck if they went over-board. We have had a great escape for which we are not half thankful enough.' There was a short peaceful interlude. 'It was quite pleasant to wake up yesterday morning and find the ship quiet, and then to look out and see that we were steaming up the beautiful harbour of Queenstown. The sun was shining, the sea quite smooth and numbers of white sailed ships dancing about and getting out of our way.

'We were soon surrounded by short boats, and the whole *Great Britain* population seemed to turn out upon Ireland. I went ashore with Mrs Bronchardt and a party of gentlemen to see what was to be seen. We had a pleasant row across the harbour and soon got to Queenstown, which is built on a sort of precipice, the white houses rising, tier upon tier, all up the hill and looking very well from a distance; but we soon got into a narrow, filthy street, swarming with children and pigs. Some parts of the town were much better, but we had soon seen all there was to see, and then we set off in a steamer for Cork.

'The sail was most beautiful between low green hills covered with woods and gentlemen's houses peeping out, or sometimes wild heathy hills and downs. We were about an hour going to Cork, which, though rather dirty, was a better town than I expected. The population generally despise bonnets and go bare-headed. We went to the Imperial Hotel and dined and then set off in a real Irish car to visit the ruin of Blarney Castle. The country round Cork is beautiful, something like Devonshire. We had a real specimen of an Irishman in the driver, who would have blarneyed the head off your shoulders, to say nothing of the money out of your purse.'

Repairs were quickly finished and the *Great Britain* sailed on 24 February 1861. Normality returned and the captain appeared at breakfast when it was learned that the storm had been worse than the one in which the *Royal Charter*, had been lost. The *Great Britain* had been saved by being out at sea while the *Charter* was caught close inshore. Only a day or two passed before Rachel Henning's grateful remembrance of the solidity of the ship was replaced by more housewifely insights: 'You cannot think how dirty everything gets: hands, clothes, everything is black. The white in my dress is in a most disastrous state. I never saw such a dirty ship. We are well supplied with water, however, and as yet no animalculae have made their appearance.'

Thomas Atkinson had a quieter start. But he had problems too. Putting the word 'Cabin' on his box had not been enough to prevent it being stowed in a hold and he had to make a quick dash to Liverpool to get some extra items until the hold was opened a week at sea. 'Got under weigh and steamed slowly down the Mersey closely followed by the tender—crowds of people lining each side of the river and the docks—shouting and waving—tho' a considerable number bestowed their attention on a couple of American-bound steamers on the point of starting—on clearing the Rock Light we dipped the ensign and fired a gun frightening everyone in an absurd manner.

'I saw my mate "Westly" in the Cabin for the first time—he seems a nice sort of fellow and I only hope we get on well together—he is going out to join his brother on a sheep station at Wagga Wagga. He likewise is in a fix about his boxes—in fact in a great deal worse plight not even having a tooth brush.'

On the fourth day out 'we had a notice this morning that the luggage would be overhauled—giving passengers an opportunity to get out fresh clothing—my box having been stowed away most stupidly among the cargo somewhere it could not be found—I had to borrow till tomorrow—wind light all day—not moving more than eight knots. Tuesday 17th [August 1869]. No luggage again today—very annoying—beginning to think it has not come on board—men hunting all day for my particular box—playing quoits and Bull—reading, smoking, etc etc. Captain makes himself most agreeable to everybody—even among the 2nd Class passengers.

Wednesday 18th. Captain told me this morning—my box

could not be found but that if I liked I could go down and look myself—which I did—scrambling about over endless boxes in a dark hold for half an hour with several sailors, mates, etc. but it was no use. The mate said it was possible it might be in the forehold—but not likely—but I said I would search any possible place—accordingly we descended into the bowels of the ship in the forecastle—going down endless ladders and at last arriving in a terrible black stinking hold where even with the assistance of several glowing lanterns little could be seen tho' much felt and smelt. We scrambled about over a chaotic mass of boxes of all sorts and sizes for upwards of half an hour and were just giving up in despair when my box was discovered stored away at the bottom of a heap of others in a dark corner. I felt considerably relieved.'

On the next day William Molyneux's diary shows that the steerage passengers were still not wholly settled. 'On deck about six, the sun perceptibly warmer. The awning spread over the deck. Nearly boiled to death carrying the beds and linen on deck to air them—and then had the carpenter down to alter the berths to make a little more room.

'After which we had to scour the place out—you would laugh to have seen me on my hands and knees scrubbing away, perspiration running down. Captain Gray on his rounds caught me at it with Betsy laughing at me. He asked her if she belonged to me and said it was what every man ought to do on board ship. After that I was washing handkerchiefs. It took till after dinner when it was so hot that neither cared to go on deck—me in shirt sleeves without waistcoat.'

Rachel Henning was 'very much afraid we shall not put in at St Vincent's . . . the passengers say that she never stops anywhere now.' This was not, however, an invariable rule. The *Great Britain* stopped at St Vincent in the Cape Verde Islands on her second trip to Australia which began—after she had been altered to three-masted full ship rig—on 11 August 1853, and she called there in 1867 when John McLennan was aboard.

One of the passengers in 1853 was Richard Newhall, aged 23, of Birmingham, who married Sarah Morris against her parents' wishes and was packed off to see if he could expand the family pin, needle, and hairpin business in Australia. In his diary he notes: 'I am Happy to say that Sarah is injoyon beter Health then Ever her did in Her Life—But I told you I ad not Solde

Eny of the goods but I altred my mind during the time we stopt at Senvino. We Stopt three Days at Senvino and I went on Shore and Took Sarah with me—and I did a small Trad with them—and I got Sevrale Bottles of Port wine and Madarra wine—which I found to be very usefull on the Voige for Sarah. But those Pepol are all Black and go quit Naked for the bigest Part of them—so it was quit a new sight for us to see. But the Place is very poor. But when we came Back to the Ship we had the Pleasure of seeing a Large Shark caught and Killed by the Passengers and I Helped to Draw Him up out of the Water my Selfe ... the one caught was about 20 feet Long.'

When the 1853 voyagers crossed the Equator on 3 September they had, wrote Richard Newhall, 'a jolly bit of fun with the Saylers for they began to shave all the Stewards and all the Saylors that ad not been over the Line befor. But they do Not Shave the Passengers at all and the Wether was very fine and very warm for we have not ad so much as too oures raine up to this time. But as regards the *Great Britain* Steam Ship qualitys they are first rate for the rufer the Sea the beter Her Seems to Stand it and the liven is as good as can be Expected for the Voige we allways ad Nuts and rasons on a Sunday which often put us in mind of things we use to get at home. But have wished meny a time we ad got Some of the grapes out of the green House. But me and Sarah often got together and ad our glass of wine and Talked about what you used to Tel us at night after us ad don work—But I must Tel you that Sarah gets very much lik Her Mother for Her often gives me a bit of a bloenup but I laugh at her and Tels her I dont care so her wont through nothing at me no arder than a Ball of Worsted which we often amuse oure Selfs with.'

Richard Newhall made a couple of friends on the trip, one a lawyer's son who lent the pair books to read. 'My other frind is a young man that as been out to Australia and as com home to bring out 2 moor of is brothers with him and he as been doing very well so him & Me often have a bit of a Chat about the Gold Diggins.' That friend said 'that he will go into the Needles trade for E think he can do well at it'. There was 'Plenty of Musice and Dancing & Singin Every day so that it Passes the time away very well.

'Theare was a Grand Ball given by the Captin [Barnard Mathews] and he Songe Several good songs theare was Plenty of good Singin & Musice and Dancing and it was kept up till next morning but the best sight that I like is to go and Sit on the Bow Sprite of the Ship of a nice moon Light night it is beautifull to See Her Plow through the Sea at the rate of 15 Nots per oure.'

John McLennan arrived at St Vincent on Boxing Day 1867 where the *Great Britain* took on coal. 'During that time the natives was out with their little boats load of oranges and all kinds of fruit, their was some of them also good at diving, as the People crowded to the side of the ship to see them, they would cry, massa tro sixpence in de water me catch it if any would thro one, he would dive after it, he would come up with it Laughing ha ha massa me got it, they would swim near as fast as a shark. On the 27th about 4 o'clock we left cape verde islands, and the sailors under the command of Captain Gray, was not long in setting sail with the aid of a great many of the passengers that enjoyed themselves in helping to pull the ropes.'

On New Year's Day John McLennan crossed the Equator. The previous evening 'their was a lot of us that stopped up till 12 o'clock watching to Bring the new year in, when it struck 12 the bells rang, and the captain came up and thanked them, wanted them to sing God save the Queen, and go all to bed. Finished by singing 3 cheers to capt. and crew, you would laugh to hear some of the Irish talking about crossing the line they actually thought they would see it.'

Eight days later 'all the steerage single men passengers was ordered to take up their beds, and get them aired, their is certain days set aside for the purpose, and Bills stuck up so as to let all such parties know, and the doctor attends to see that they all attend to the orders, and keepe their rooms clean as well.... (11th) ... today the sailors month is up so they make it a day of sport for themselves they acted a play called the cast away of the dead horse, they Got themselves Blackened and dressed as Funny as they could they got the shape of a horse made of canvas, they put him in a box with wheels on it, they put a man on the horse back, dressed like a Negro chief, a crown on his head.

'Some of them Pulled it round the deck, and others acted as Bobbys some Musisioners they had 2 Unicorns two fiddlers a drumer & triangle, they marched around the deck three times with the dead horse, which pleased the lookers on very well. They had a block fixed to the end of the fore yard runn a rope through it tied it to the dead horse they hoisted the horse and the chief up to the end of the yard amid the cheers, so the chief having a knife cut the rope below him and the horse fell and he was lored back to deck so that was the castaway, three cheers was given to the dead Horse, and they made 2 live horses of 4 men, they put rugs on them and went through the same perform-ance afterwards they had a dance, sung some negro songs, and was over after three cheers.'

In his description of the same event almost exactly four years later Henry Weatherburn, aged 22, a 2nd class passenger from Leicester, put the number of participants at ten—'some like plough boys, some black women, and 2 as quack doctors with false beards selling "medical comforts" to passengers ... they halted occasionally to dance and sing accompanied by a fiddle. Dinah's dancing was much appreciated which resulted in a collection being taken among the passengers.'

Henry Weatherburn explained that the pantomime 'The Dead Horse' was performed one month out from port because 'the sailors draw one month's pay before commencing the voyage and this is usually spent before leaving port'. It was usually spent in payment for lodgings and other comforts supplied to seamen by lodging house keepers who were frequently the doubtful agents and protectors of sailors ashore—giving them a roof over their heads, finding them new ships, and generally managing their affairs in such a way that the Dead Horse pantomime often marked for sailors a genuine liberation from home-port ex-ploitation.

For the saloon passengers these diversions were not enough. Thomas Atkinson was on the verge of boredom. A fortnight out, 'after tea myself and several other—4 young ladies and a young fellow got up an impromptu charade—"Message" being the word—in which I took a rather prominent part in the last scene —as I was retiring rather gracefully I fell backwards over a water can accidentally which brought forth some hearty laughter the audience fancying it was done purposely'. Even so, he writes next day, 'if it were not for the frequency of eating it is impossible to say what one would do.' A couple of days later this reflection is echoed: 'The passengers have been speaking about the absence of all fun and attempts to enliven the voyage which is very true—and I was told by a Lady that I was looked upon as the mainstay and only hope—such an astonishing assertion that I have felt sorely puzzled for I never in my life took part especially a leading part in any such kind of thing—however I have come to the conclusion that I must take an active part in everything.'

This determination was not new for he recorded only the day before: 'Several of us have been talking about a Concert and Christy Minstrel entertainment after crossing the line—so tonight we had a preliminary meeting, myself among the number altho' I can't sing except in a chorus and can't play any instrument—yet if everybody was to shirk out for the same reason there would be no one left—we act in the boudoir and had a noisy meeting rather—Westly to take the Bones being rather funny and fully stored with niggerisms and myself to manage "Sambo"—we can manage to raise a penny whistle concertina—guitar—piano—tambourine—and a comb and paper.'

Next day he stuck up a notice announcing the chess championship of the *Great Britain*, had a Christy Minstrel meeting where songs were chosen 'after which we had a very jolly dance on deck—a set of quadrilles, a gallop, Lancers, and the Sir Roger all of which I danced.' This positive activity did not inhibit a rather negative comment on the following Sunday: 'The RCs having their service at 9 conducted by a man named Maloney—a blasphemous individual and certainly not fit for the duty tho' I dare say he satisfies his congregation.' He undertook the duty of clerk at the Anglican service where the preacher's voice—a Mr Morrell—was too weak and nervous for much of the sermon to be heard. 'The Scotch service at 2.30 which I also attended.'

In the following week the chess championship begins, there is another dance, and an entertainment consisting of tableaux vivants and charades is arranged. On Tuesday there was some spontaneous fun: 'We were rather alarmed at seeing a Lady passenger (Mrs Carter) coming round with a list for subscriptions —which we soon found out to be for the child that was born a day or two ago. No sooner however was the fact discovered that the gentlemen department simultaneously dispersed in all directions—a most ludicrous scene—I took refuge in a signal chest, the lid only half shutting down upon me—but I was found out and ignominiously drawn forth with flags wrapped round me.'

On Friday a small cloud appeared to qualify the tone of these activities at an afternoon practice for a concert in which Thomas

Atkinson was to take the tenor part in a quartet—'there is a nasty feeling owing to one Lady having assumed command to the dissatisfaction of the greater number and there is every prospect of the thing falling to the ground.' Next day however enough progress was made to form a committee for the concert when:

'Mr Smith went out and came in again and said it was the wish of some of the Ladies that the committee should only consist of married people—such an absurd idea and so bluntly and rudely said that Mr Morrell immediately resigned as did Miss Holmes. Some hot words passed between Smith and Morrell, the former a vulgar individual who had been allowed too much latitude at first. The meeting however, and concert came to an untimely end, and in the course of the afternoon some warm language took place between Smith and Morrell resulting in a very unfriendly feeling likely to last to the end of the voyage.'

Next day (Sunday 5 September) after another disappointing sermon from Morrell, 'the chief subject of conversation was yesterday's little fracas—general opinion going against Mrs Carter who was very rude to Miss Holmes before anything was said about the concert—submitted a programme for Mrs Carter's approval who wouldn't look at it saying she had arranged one herself—it seems strange that such little disagreeableness should occur to mar the otherwise pleasant course of feeling. At eight o'clock had service in the steerage a small poky place hung round with lamps and being very low there was a very unpleasant lamp odor.'

On Monday another fractious meeting took place at which there was 'another break out—one lady would not sing if another sang and so on, and at last the captain said he should not allow such a thing as a concert to take place if such feeling existed'. That day's entry began 'still screw—screw—screwing along, and no wind'. A couple of days later 'the wind commenced to get fresher and the ship rolled tremendously and about 7 o'clock this morning we were all roused up on deck by some fearful crashing and banging. The captain, officers, boatswain, and men all shouting at the tops of their voices and on reaching the deck a terrible state of confusion and wreck. In the first place the jib-boom had gone, carried away a few feet from the deck—a splendid spar as we had occasion to observe when looking at it on the deck afterwards.

'A dreadful loss and we had to bear away direct east nearly

before the wind, the ship not steering without the jibs. The next important loss was the stunsail boom of the foremast which went with a bang going completely through the rigging and everything without doing any damage right out clear of the ship sinking and coming up again like a bottle, the next loss was the splitting into ribbons of the main togallantsail which was flying and making about in all directions. That was about all and quite enough too. It was a severe loss—steam was got up to keep her as near the course as possible. The captain naturally was greatly put out—this was the second jib boom he had ever lost, and this one had been in the ship for the last ten years or so. The crew were hard at work repairing the damage for the rest of the day.'

In spite of the frictions in the saloon the charades, tableaux, and Christy Minstrel shows were put on, and of the minstrels— who did 'The Old Kentucky Home', 'Dancing Mad', 'Doo Dah', and an extravaganza 'The Haunted Lane'—Thomas Atkinson commented, 'It was very gratifying to find that our entertainment was well appreciated—we were well blacked with burnt cork and oil but I had least on and more resembled a mulatto than a bona fide nigger.'

Disagreements in steerage were less obscure than in the saloon, as John McLennan records: '21st [January 1868]. Fair wind today their was 2 young Irishmen put in jail for being riotous and annoying the rest of the Passengers.' Two days later: 'It's very cold today, their was a row in the third cabin yesterday between two women one was married and she was for thrashing the other one for winking at her husband, this same woman, cast out with her man at the New Year, and she swore that he did not do her over for the last fortnight, a Laugh.'

On the 25th: 'Fair wind today, we Passed a yankee whalefisher, as she was lying too, we was pritty close on her, we could see them burning down the last one they caught. I saw two of the firemen fighting about some frivalous affair, the one knocked the other down twice, and they dropped it, so the one that was beat wanted to fight with knives, but the other would not do it, another man laid up by the measles, From the Second Cabin. 26th. A strong breeze and a heavy sea running, their was a wife delivered of 2 youngsters last night in the steerage, it is too cold today to keep divine Service on deck, so the English service is to be kept in the first cabin. Cathlics in the Steerage, and Presbyterian in second cabin, one of the sailors quarrled with the first

Mate, he was taken to Jail, but he got out in about 4 hours. 27th. Their is another Birth today, the 2 that was born on the 26th is dead, another man from the Second cabin laid up with the Measles, their was a sailor hurt by a fall as they were taking down the fore Stan sail, but he wasent much hurt. 28th. It calmed last night so they were forced to get up steam about 12 o'clock, two men quarrled in the 3rd class, one of them was drunk, 4 of the officers was taking him to prison and the gangway was so slipry he got rid of them, so he was not put in. 29th. The steam is off today. Their was two men put in jail from the second cabin, for being drunk, and annoying the rest of the passengers, one of them pushed [pissed?] in his Birth and the other shit his bed, and when the purser came to look after them, he held out his hand full of dirt to shake hands with him, I believe their is something remarkable about this ship every day.'

All this ship-board interest kept John McLennan writing steadily through to the end of the trip. Other diarists generally grew weary. Thomas Atkinson lapsed into silence for the last five days. Ivor Josiah Williams, returning to Warrnambool, Victoria, on the voyage that began on 17 December 1871, is reduced by 11 February 1872 to 'General drunkeness at 10 pm last night. 12th. Beautifully fine. 13th. A general drunk, no sleep. 14th. Beam wind laying over, drunk again at the end of our saloon, no sleep. 18th. The valve of the pipes which feed the engine with water got out of order causing an hours delay. Strong head wind. Caught an albatross. 20th. Last night. General drunk.' Earlier on the same voyage Henry Weatherburn says, 'This evening we had a discussion on Intoxicating Drinks, total abstinence, prohibition etc which I think did some good and enlightened the darkness of some folk'. Not for long apparently.

Henry Weatherburn is the only journal-keeper interested enough to go into the engine room of the *Great Britain* which he did on Boxing Day 1871. 'Today for the first time we were able to use a quantity of canvas—wind being in our favour. Today I went down to see the Engines and Boilers. Ship carries 1,400 tons of coal—400 tons have been used since leaving Liverpool. There are 4 boilers with 4 furnaces to each. Engines are a large pair of oscillating cylinders $82\frac{1}{2}$ inches diameter, 6 feet stroke, Fly wheel 15 feet diameter (iron teeth) which drives the main shaft 17 inches diameter to the end of which is attached screw propeller.'

John McLennan, in spite of his setting-out bottle of beer, keeps both head and eyes clear. His journal contains a temperance lecture written over nine closely packed pages to which, he adds, 'I hope the reader will pay particular attention'.

William Molyneux mentions food more often than any other *Great Britain* diarist—'Had breakfast of tea', and 'breakfast—boiled beef and coffee'. He struck a characteristically philosophic note on 18 August 1869: 'Rose half past five—on deck six—looked after breakfast being cooked. Bought some bacon and Betsy and self made the best breakfast since coming on board. It reminded us more of home. Nothing like being aboard ship to sharpen the appetite and make you glad to eat what on shore would be sent away.'

Rachel Henning had some early misgivings. 'They do not feed you so well on board this ship as they did in the *Calcutta*. There is a quantity of food, but it is coarse; great joints of pork and underdone mutton and chiefly cold. However, the first day is not a fair sample, and when the captain is on board and we are fairly off no doubt all will go smoother.'

John McLennan gives a reminder that though perhaps cold and lumpen, at least what went on the saloon table was fresh. '28th [December 1867]. Nothing to be seen today but the wide ocean a smart breeze of wind, their is 2 men shearing some of the sheep we have about 150 in all, and 50 Pigs, they kills 3 to 4 sheep every day for the cabin passengers usage.'

On the 2nd [February 1868], 'they had to get up the steam last night at 11 o'clock but its off today at 12 noon, you know they can get up the steam any time in about 3 quarters of an hour. 3rd. We are 50 days out now, its not so cold today, I expect it will be getting a little warmer they have put on the steam this morning again, the captain is very anxious to make the voyage as quick as possible, their is one young fellow I have noticed, that drunk and gambled all his money and clothes, so he is turned out a shoe black, a penny a head, in Fact their is plenty as bad as him, their was a while that their was nothing but raffles on watches, rings, merseum [meerschaum] pipes, cigars, Unicorns, clothes and everything they raffled to get money they would drink, so you may guess what sort of People we have got on board the Briton. 4th: they kept a concert in the 3rd cabin last night, and it was opened precisely at half past seven PM their was no admittance for any but 3rd class passengers. 5th: a nice breeze today, the steam was put off this morning again, the sailors is busy airing the ropes and cleaning the ship for the landing, they want to have everything as tidy as they can for the health officer Inspector.

'6th: we held a meeting in the steerage today, for the purpose of making up a petition of thanks to be given to the Captain, as a token of our respect to him, for the energies he used, towards the health and cleanliness, of the warrant passengers, 4 men made up the petition and it was read before the meeting it was unanimously approved off, and its to be sent in towards the end of the week. Also 2 men were appointed by the comitee, for to relate to Mr Campbell, our heart felt thanks to him, for his kindness and civility to us during the voyage, as it is the Captains General rule, to treat all the members on Board before landing, we were served out today with an allowance of rum hott, But the cabin passengers they Gets a different treat, But he expects something for it I believe they made a collection for him worth 70£, the wind died away, and they were forced to put on steam.

'7th they took up the screw this morning, their came a strong Breeze Of Westerly wind, about bed time, too chaps fell a-fighting, and the one broke the others finger. 8th we have had a heavy sea running, last night and today. It has been proposed, that their should be a collection made among the Steerage and Warrant Passengers, towards our little steward, he is a very little man, about as little as I ever saw, only he has not been anyways contrary to any of us, and he was doing his best to keep things clean, which was not very easily done among such a rum lott, we were all gathered together tonight, and the secretary had got the small sum of 1£ 11s. to present to our little steward which he seemed quite Pleased with our Subscription, he gave us a short speech, he returned thanks and wished us all good luck towards our future prospects, After which we held a concert, and a good many songs were sung, it was concluded by giving cheers to the captain crew and chairman, as we expect this to be the last Saturday, on board the good ship Great Britain.

'9th fair wind, divine service was held in the second cabin, the text 14th chapter 2nd verse of Johns Epistle, after which the Reverend Minister Prayed earnestly that God might be with us during the remainder of the voyage and that we might reach the desired haven safe that He would go with every one to the many places of residence, and that all which had been spoken on this ship might Prove, effectial, to the good of many. We have got [an]other 2 Births.

'10th Fine weather today, we are expecting to arrive at Melbourne tomorrow, their is two of the firemen laid up with the Measles.

'11th last night we had a concert singing went on till 10 o'clock after it was over, a great many went up on deck all in a great glee watching the first sight of land, which would be cape Ottoa [Otway] light, as it was night, but if it was day we would see land some time before that, so they were all glad that they were coming so near land. Just after they had sighted the light on their Port Bough, I was in bed myself and I heard the machinery going at an unusual pace, when I perceived that the steam was put off, I instantly understood their was something wrong by the way it shook the ship like an explosion, but we have reason to be thankful, that it was nothing serious, it was some Joint that the shaft that drives the screw, that broke, you may consider the confusion that it caused among them all, at first no one knew what might be the matter, you would see some of them running up half naked, and them that was up running down telling she was sinking, their was [a man] I laughed at, he got his one leg in his trousers but he hadent time to get in the other, and the other fellow that put his shirt on wrong he put the back to the front and the collar was sticking all up about his face. When I rose next morning, I could see we was pritty close on land, with a dead calm, the tide was driving her nearer the shore, the smiths was busy working, but we was helpless wanting wind or steam, we fired 3 cannons so that they would telegraph from the lighthouse to Melbourne, you will know that a cannon on the outside of the baar is a sign of distress, about 12 noon we spied a steam in the distance coming in towards us, we was not long when we observed that it was the mails that left on the 20th December, they fired one cannon first then other 2, when he came to know it was the Great Britain he kept away, he did not want to be hindered by us especially as Captain Gray was trying to beat the mails, and so we would only for the accident.

'However by 3 in the afternoon, they were enabled to start the engines at half speed. 12th last night after we started we only had half speed but they got it up stronger during the night, I got up about 3 in the morning to see Port Phillips heads. The Pilot was on board he had come by a small boat, we was then 7 miles on the outside of the heads also 2 steam tugs had come up then who was coming to our rescue, after getting the Telegram, but Captain Gray told them he would manage himself, and they turned Back, the distance between cape Ottoa and Port Phillips heads is 60 miles, between the heads and Melbourne is 40 miles, after we got inside of the heads, they fired a gun, as is usually done, and then we hove too and anchored until the health officer came on board after a little discussion the order was given to hoist anchor, and proceded, I could give you no description that would lead you to understand anything as the way the land lies its not very hilly, and its full of Bush all around you can see a few wooden huts here and there, you would not think much about living in them, we went round about the bay into Melbourne.

'I saw a few small boats fishing with lines, and they seemed to be getting as much as they could take in, little fish about the size of whitings. When we was coming close to our anchorage, the Emigrant Inspector came on board by steam tug, all our names was called over, and he asked if we had any complaints or if we got Plenty to eat and drink everyone would answer yes of course, But some of the Irish boys would come on, yes sur, arra but we got plenty, Peas soop, and rice and Plum duff and everything sur.

'We arrived the ancharage at miday, the cabin passengers was put ashore first, and any one that could pay a boat to take them ashore would go, but we did not get ashore till next day they put us up by the steamer to the queens wharf at Melbourne, that is nine miles up river we was landed at the warf ourselves and luggage at miday on the 13th ult.'

In 1869 too it was a fine day at the close of the voyage. Thomas Atkinson rallied to his 'Partridge and Coopers Patent Improved Metallic Book. Warranted if written on with their prepared pencils to be as durable as ink. 192 Fleet Street Corner of Chancery Lane EC.' With his prepared pencil (proved now to be as durable as ink) he entered: 'Monday Oct 11th We are now in the most lovely weather bright, clear, and fresh with a glorious smooth sea—saw a tolerably large whale for the first time in my life. Today was the captain's gala day—he giving a dinner—Champagne etc—a Testimonial was presented to him accompanied by a purse of £65. 10s. Mr Waterhouse proposed his health in a very appropriate speech—and the jolly old

Captain replied in a very characteristic manner. The bachelors brought down shame on themselves by allowing the Captain to propose the health of the Ladies, replied to by Mr Young.'

Only Rachel Henning takes us down the gangplank and ashore. In May 1861: 'We spent one day seeing Melbourne, its shops and streets and grand buildings, and a very fine town it is, far better than Sydney. Another day we went up the river to the Botanic Garden and Zoological Gardens, and another we made a picnic to a place called Gardener's Creek, about seven miles up the Yarra Yarra.

'You cannot think how kind the captain was to me during the voyage and especially during my stay in Melbourne. He always took me under his especial care in all the boating and railway travelling backwards and forwards, for we had to go up by rail to the town; the ship was lying about a quarter of an hour's pull from Sandridge pier, and then there was about a quarter of an hour's journey by rail to Melbourne. I was very sorry to say good-bye to the *Great Britain* and her captain when we sailed from Melbourne. She is a splendid ship and I am sure we all have reason to speak well of her.'

While at sea Rachel Henning claimed that the Captain said he preferred sitting at the head of her table in the saloon—he headed tables in turn. 'We had,' she says, 'far more fun going on at our table than at any of the others.' Nonetheless, 'somehow there was a good deal of stiffness and party feeling on board the ship. I hardly know how it arose, but half the people were not friendly with the other half.'

Only one all-embracing theory has been proposed to explain the stresses revealed by the *Great Britain* passengers' diaries—it was due to the use of steam. In his book *The Colonial Clippers* Mr Basil Lubbock, devotee of pure sailing ships, draws this inference from goings-on aboard the *Great Britain*'s sister ship in the Eagle Line. 'The ill-fated *Royal Charter*'s passage home in the summer of 1856 presents an example of a badly run and disciplined ship. The food was bad, everyone had a growl about something, drunken riots occurred constantly, fighting in which even the crew and stewards took a part was of almost daily occurrence and excessive gambling ruined scores of returning diggers on the lower deck. I am glad to say that I can find no such instance of disorder and lack of discipline amongst the ships which relied upon sail power alone.'

CHAPTER VII

Home and Dry

'Her grim dereliction dominated the scene. It was perhaps not altogether extraordinary that my first sight of this old hulk had instantly put me in mind of the scabrous old crones who sat match-selling outside the dock gates of the English seaports. She had the same look of decrepitude, broken-down fineness; not so much the air of lost youth, as a terrible emanation of the lost beauty of old age. The vulgarity of her sawn-down bowsprit reminded me of the pendulous indecency of these old women's noses.

'She must have been a three-masted ship for I saw that although grossly amputated her fore, main, and mizzen masts were still standing; on the main mast, starkly disproportionate, hung a huge spar, by the look of it her original lower main yard-arm. She was used as a wool store hulk. I saw she was rolling unpleasantly to her over-sized moorings, showing off her streaked and naked-looking body; as I continued to stare at her I was reminded even more forcibly of the derelict dock-gate match-sellers. Her moored idleness emphasised with tragic exactitude the role of barren uselessness. As she rolled and displayed her worn out charms I thought there was about her a hint of the disillusioned bitter hostility that emanated from the diseased old women.'

That was how the *Great Britain* looked through the eyes of a merchant navy cadet in 1914. Harold Owen, brother of Wilfred Owen, goes on in *Journey from Obscurity* to describe a nightmare adolescent crisis stranded aboard the ship among the wool bales in a terrible storm. For the only time the ship is in the hands of a powerful imaginative writer and she emerges as a malignant relic. To the people of the Falkland Islands however she became only an unchanging part of the scenery—where men in Stanley went to work as men elsewhere went to factories and offices, and which visitors to the capital remembered as part of the scenery, like an old castle in a medieval town. She was always there, but never remarked on, honourably retired, but harder worked than ever.

In 1905 there was an unusual flurry of interest when the former manager at the GWSSCo yard under Mr Paterson came forward—at the age of 89—and gave Lloyds' chief surveyor in Cardiff a model of the ship. The foreman, Mr Thomas Hooper, said that it was the working model, made by him, from which the *Great Britain* had been built. Lloyds' reached down its *Great Britain* file and sent out to Stanley for news of the ship, followed by requests for pictures. These came with apologies for the retarded state, in the Falklands, of 'the art of photographing'.

During the early 1930s, as she fell into total disuse, thoughtful people wondered what should be done with the ship. The Falkland Island Company made an offer of the ship to the Government. Sir Henniker Heaton, governor of the islands, was about to raise an appeal to have her taken back to England for preservation; the first call for funds was to have coincided with the 50th anniversary—25 May 1936—of the *Great Britain*'s last arrival in Stanley. But a survey indicated that it would cost £10,000 or more just to preserve her—never mind tow her back to Bristol. This was thought too much. Then the Royal Navy was to sink her out at sea—an order the Navy is said to have jibbed at. There was a plan to use her as a bridge over a creek, which was impracticable

It was finally decided to do what the harbour master had predicted—tow her away and beach her. The last home of the *Great Britain* was to be Sparrow Cove, an indentation on the north side of the channel leading from Stanley west to the sea. She was towed out on 12 April 1937, holes were knocked in her bottom, and she was left to disintegrate. Her centenary went by in the middle of the war with a minor-key eulogy from a writer in the Falklands in a commemorative booklet: 'Now she rests a great lady and very frail, but still beautiful, in the land-locked place of Sparrow Cove. On a fine day when the sea and sky are blue her old timbers gratefully absorb the warmth, and glow grey and amber against the honey coloured grass and she rouses herself from sleep to tell tales of the Antipodes and the windy Horn to respectful deputations from the penguin rookery on the hill above the cove.'

In spite of her age, the *Great Britain* contributed to the war effort against Hitler. Mrs Rose Wilkinson, chairman of the Red

Cross Society in the Falklands, recalls that 'a great deal, if not
all the suitable wood was dismantled from the hulk and made
voluntarily by carpenters of the FICo into small tables, lamps,
etc., which were auctioned by the Red Cross. They made a
substantial sum which was sent home. I myself procured an
elegant greenheart pedestal fruit bowl for 14 guineas but it
was the only one made as the wood proved too difficult to turn.'
Bits of the ship had been vanishing as raw material for the
memento trade since she arrived, and she was dispersed world
wide in many shapes—from a bedside lamp in Weybridge
Surrey, to the conductor's baton in the ship's band on HMS
Sussex.

Innocent depredations have been matched by other uninten-
tional perils. In March 1968 a keen type aboard HMS *Protector*,
ice patrol ship in the South Atlantic, conceived the idea of an
exercise in which the Falklands had been invaded (presumably
by the Argentinians). A party of sailors was sent off to investigate
lights seen on the hill above Sparrow Cove. The group's radios
were taken aboard the *Great Britain*—seen dimly in the darkness by the light of shielded torches. There was a freezing wind
and sleet and a member of the party remembers 'someone
suggested lighting a fire out of some of the old timbers—but this
would have given away our position ... we didn't realise that
someone's dream could have been ruined had we made the fire
to keep warm'.

By the time it was decided not to light that fire the first steps
towards making the dream a reality had already been taken.
Three men came together, each with a distinctive contribution,
to make the recovery of the *Great Britain* as swift and effective
an archaeological commando raid as is ever likely to be seen. Dr
Ewan Corlett, aged 45, a consultant naval architect, was the first
mover. Mr Richard Goold-Adams, aged 55, son of a former
Governor of Queensland, was the second, and 'Union' Jack Hayward, engineering company director, Bahamas property
developer, and Anglophile extraordinary, was the last.

It was a letter to *The Times*, the last one on the page, which
unpretentiously started the ball rolling on 9 November 1967:
'The first iron built ocean going steamship, and the first such
ship to be driven entirely by propeller was the *Great Britain*
designed and launched by Isambard Kingdom Brunel. This, the
forefather of all modern ships, is lying a beached hulk in the

Falkland Islands at this moment. The *Cutty Sark* has rightly been preserved at Greenwich and HMS *Victory* at Portsmouth. Historically the *Great Britain* has an equal claim to fame and yet nothing has been done to document the hulk, let alone recover it and preserve it for record. May I make a plea that the authorities should at least document, photograph, and fully record this wreck, and at best do something to recover the ship and place her on display as one of the very few really historic ships still in existence?'

Dr Corlett said that he came to write that letter in this way: 'Twenty years ago I was the naval architect to the British Aluminium Company, and when I left they presented me with a copy of a print of the *Great Britain*. Over the years my interest in the ship inspired by this print developed—and I also happened to inherit all the copies of *Sea Breezes* from scratch, an enormously interesting magazine, especially the early volumes. I researched her up in these; as a naval architect I was particularly interested in her place in marine history, and it snowballed until eventually I felt inspired to do something about it. So I wrote to *The Times*. To my surprise this produced a considerable amount of correspondence.'

Richard Goold-Adams was one of the people who didn't see the letter. His first conscious memory of the ship was seeing a picture of her in *The Observer* with a caption describing a vague plan to try to bring her home. This seemed to him to be 'a worthwhile thing to do'. As founder and chairman of the Institute of Strategic Studies, a considerable writer and broadcaster, and director of the Guthrie Corporation (Malayan palm oil and rubber), he found that he 'still had a little time unused' and tried to find out more about the *Great Britain* and its rescue. The name of the ship more than anything else fixed it in his mind. His inquiries, and connections established through the newspaper letter, resulted in a meeting on 5 April 1968 at the London offices of the Falkland Island Company in Pall Mall. Only four people were present—Dr Corlett, Mr Basil Greenhill, director of the National Maritime Museum, Mr J. H. Yorath, a director of the FICo, and Richard Goold-Adams. Here the germ of the salvage was created.

During the summer of 1968 Richard Goold-Adams and Ewan Corlett got to know one another better. A committee was formed —or 'project' to use the preferred name—with Richard Goold-

Adams in the chair; lines of communication were already out to Buckingham Palace where Prince Philip was known to be interested, and to the Ministry of Defence which could offer nothing but 'a sympathetic hearing'.

The SS *Great Britain* Project came into being as an off-shoot of the Society for Nautical Research which simplified its registration as a charity.

The Americans who had seen the ship—they were not technically qualified—told Ewan Corlett that they thought the *Great Britain* was just a shell of rust with no strength anywhere; other lay reports said the same. He ordered from a Falklands photographer—the art had advanced—several hundred pictures of the ship taken from as many angles as possible. 'I subjected these to a technical analysis during 1968 and came to the conclusion that she probably was not as bad as people said.' But Ewan Corlett wanted to do a proper survey before any firm dispositions about recovery were attempted. 'I wanted,' he said, 'to combine the approach of the marine archaeologist and the marine surveyor.' The promised sympathy of the Ministry of Defence was invoked and a place was found aboard the new ice patrol vessel, *Endurance*, shortly outbound on a political mission to the Falklands aimed at reducing Anglo-Argentine friction about the islands. This passage allowed Dr Corlett five days' work without having to spend a month on the Islands—the interval of passages by sea; there is no air service.

Volunteers from *Endurance* gave a hand, learned how to use the ultra-sonic thickness tester for examining the hull above water and left others—normally the party was five strong—plotting water depths around the ship, measuring the thickness of mud with a portable echo-sounder, and diving under the ship as deeply as possible to assess her underwater portions. In the report he wrote when he got home Dr Corlett concluded that the ship was salvable, that general wastage was of the order of 40 per cent, there were water holes, of course, but that generally she was capable of salvage and could be salvaged for about £150,000. But there was a time limit. From the bottom of the huge square hole cut in her starboard side for the wool bales a crack had developed; resting on a shifting sand bed the *Great Britain*'s back was in danger of breaking. She had to be recovered, Dr Corlett estimated, within five years.

The sympathetic ear at the Ministry of Defence belonged to

Mr David Owen, MP for a Plymouth constituency. Richard Goold-Adams was talking to him about something else in the early summer of 1969 when Owen—who was Under-Secretary of State for the Navy—said that Jack Hayward had just given enough money to buy Lundy Island and might be interested in supporting the *Great Britain* project.

Contact was made and Jack Hayward visited the Goold-Adams' flat near Paddington and after a two-hour talk during which the cost was put at between £75,000 and £150,000 he said 'Provided it costs no more than that I'll take care of it'. Richard Goold-Adams couldn't believe that he had heard correctly and asked to hear the words again. Then—because Jack Hayward is not one for putting this kind of thing in writing—he said 'What if you die?' His wife had instructions to honour his commitments. From that moment the rescue became not a matter of long term fund-raising, but immediate action.

United Towing Company of Hull was approached—Jack Hayward was overjoyed because its tug *Englishman* would do the job—and sent three men to the Falklands to estimate the job. They came back with a gloomy report, summarised by the managing director of the company as: 'We were advised that the condition of the SS *Great Britain* was such that she could be towed back to this country on her own bottom once temporary repairs had been affected. In our opinion this was definitely not the case.' Stories of lightly tapping through the *Great Britain*'s hull to salt water, and a matchbox full of sawdust from the rotten masts, added weight to this conclusion—a conclusion which Ewan Corlett continues to oppose; he thinks that the ship could have been brought back on her own bottom filled with plastic foam.

The day after the contents of the report were known, the three leaders of the project were to go to Brunel University, West London, to take part in a television film about the recovery of the ship in which they all all pretended that the plans were as before. 'It was a bit strained,' said Jack Hayward.

There was a meeting with United Towing at which the two viewpoints were debated. The project, on the basis that the towing company's figures did not match measurements being taken for it in the Falklands, rejected their conclusion. But project figures showed that the crack had become 20 per cent wider—'it was clear that my estimate of breaking up in five years was a hideously accurate one; it was,' said Ewan Corlett, 'an optimistic one, not a pessimistic one.' As a token of how near the end might be the project at this time—December 1969—had the main mast stayed. It had begun to come loose—it would cut right through the ship if it fell.

Dr Corlett was then authorised to discuss the recovery with the Southampton salvage firm of Risdon Beazley. It had for some time—unknown to the project—been closely associated with the Hamburg firm Ulrich Harms, which had pioneered for four years the pontoon recovery method. From the first meeting of Dr Corlett and the managing director of Risdon Beazley, Mr Alan Crothall, on 29 December everything fell into place. By 11 January the timetable had been completely fixed, technical schedules worked out, and costs agreed. All on the basis of the Corlett report.

Mr Leslie O'Neil, Risdon Beazley's chief salvage officer—upon whose word, finally, these arrangements would depend—was sent to the Falklands to do another survey, and returned with a view that confirmed Ewan Corlett's estimate of a four-to-one chance of success. There was a pontoon on its way to a job in West Africa. A Dutch ship was just leaving for the Falklands from London, and there was just time to get pumping and other equipment aboard. The rescue had started—a rescue made possible by the pontoon, a great steel mattress 240 ft. by 80 ft. by 15ft. divided into 15 compartments and controlled whether sunk, or high out of the water, by compressed air.

Only one difficulty marred this providential change in the fortunes of the project—Jack Hayward's stipulation about all-British enterprise. At the very outset he had been told about a possible Greek tug to which his answer had been: 'Not on your nelly; don't associate me with any Greek tug, in fact any tug of any nationality but British. If this succeeds you can imagine what the cartoonists and publicity people would say if the *Great Britain* comes home towed by a dirty old Greek tug.' Both the *Varius 2* tug and the *Mulus 3* pontoon were German. Jack Hayward said he agreed to go forward with them providing they were re-registered in Britain before they entered British waters. This was not done and feelings were a little frayed about it.

It was mid-March 1970 when the salvage party, five English, 15 Germans, assembled by sea and air in Montevideo. Euan Donald Howard, 4th Baron of Strathcona and Mount Royal, a man of wide interests living in the West Country and with Royal Naval and engineering experience, agreed to go with the expedition. He represented the project. This was a necessary office because the question of the ownership of the *Great Britain* was causing anxiety to the project. The vessel was a Crown wreck. The British Colonial Office said that it could be released to the project only with the permission of the Falkland Islands. Richard Goold-Adams had anxious radio-telephone talks with the Governor, Sir Cosmo Haskard, and at one stage said he nearly turned the flotilla back because permission, if given, would be accompanied by impossible conditions—like personal liability by members of the project if the recovery failed and caused a harbour obstruction.

These problems were overcome. When the salvors arrived in Port Stanley on 25 March after nine-day voyage, Lord Strathcona said that the islanders were surprised to see the party at all. 'They expected that we would stay in Port Stanley for a week or so, and discuss with them the project—very like a Scottish crofter would say "So you're going to Sparrow Cove to rescue the *Great Britain*. Now that's a considerable task...."' But they had to get over to the cove almost the next day. At the root of the opposition—apart from reflections about arbitrary plunder by the rich motherland of the poor colony—was the feeling that the plan would end only in the dismemberment of the *Great Britain*. The failure which many saw as inevitable would put an unnecessarily squalid end to the old ship.

With feelings of this kind to be assuaged, the possibility of more high-level snags, and the need to try to gather surviving bits of the *Great Britain* that had found homes ashore, the usefulness of some brisk, titled charm was clear. Lord Strathcona was also the *Daily Telegraph* and *Sunday Times* special correspondent, and one of his major achievements was a nightly broadcast on the islands' wireless giving an account of the day's progress. These thawed some reservations about the recovery. And Lord Strathcona was averse from neither paint brush nor shovel.

Before leaving South America some of the vertical posts—dolphins—between which the *Great Britain* was to ride on the pontoon had been welded to its deck; sheerlegs—makeshift cranes—had been made for lifting out the masts; rough wood had been bought to make the deck of the *Great Britain* safe to walk on. The aid of the Royal Marines under Captain Malcolm McLeod—mainly in providing a ferry service from Port Stanley to Sparrow Cove—had been promised. The two firms Risdon Beazley and Ulrich Harms merged while the recovery was in progress but their separate skills and responsibilities in the Falklands, as well as nationalities, produced two chains of command. Leslie O'Neil organised the preparation of the *Great Britain* for refloating, and the patching of the crack. Horst Kaulen, aged 33, and already 15 years in salvage, looked after the pontoon and the operation of heavy cutting gear. Close and amiable consultation was maintained between the two leaders.

Before he began the job Leslie O'Neil thought, 'It's hopeless—that's the reaction you get. But when you stay aboard this ship and you walk around and, backed by the knowledge that Dr Corlett had been down there and taken thickness tests of the underwater plating, then you thought well, it's worth a try. We don't often see the ship we have to float—they are completely immersed—so that when you see a ship as old as this one was sitting on the beach with a freeboard of about 18 feet you have the feeling—if we don't manage this first attempt then probably we'll get her on the second or third.'

Horst Kaulen's impression was: 'She looks smaller; on the charts and the pictures she looks bigger. She looks not so big it was better for me. After three or four days contact we feel much better and so we can try. The height and the top weight—that is more important than the length.' Lord Strathcona—who managed to keep a diary on top of everything else—recorded his first response in one word: 'Daunting'.

Day 1   26 April 1970
No wind at 6.30 a.m. and another sunny day. Wind had started by 8 o'clock when we left with the *Mulus* lashed alongside for Sparrow Cove. The *Mulus* anchor was dropped to the west of the *Great Britain*. The *Varius* dropped her wires whilst the *Mulus* was eased back with the help of the little FIC tug. However, whilst he was waiting off, the captain let the *Varius* drift too close to the shore and was then rather offended when he had a job getting her unstuck.

In the afternoon work started in earnest. The divers went down and inspected holes in the bulkheads for which patches have been made in wood with polythene, and soft rubber sealing edges. The job was held up when the boat engine could not be started and the same was true of the ship's compressor. All the batteries on board flat after ten days messing about at sea. Twenty marines laid a walkway over the deck—otherwise one is liable to fall through at any time. It is all quite rotten.

The ship's crew worked till 9.30 tonight moving the sheerlegs to the end of the *Mulus* and making new wire strops. We have laid a floor in the old galley deck house of the *Great Britain* and started tacking plywood round the edges to make a store-cum-warming-up room for divers.

Day 2   Good Friday

Bright sun all day. Where are all the stories of endless rain and so on? Calm but cold at 7 a.m. The wind rose to a fresh cold breeze all day, and then dropped again this evening, but our party had to stop at nightfall owing to lack of lighting. After many hours the portable air compressor was at last persuaded into life so that mud could be dug away from beneath the crack by the divers. The crew nearly finished preparing the sheerlegs in the morning whilst we got on well with temporary patching of the old deckhouse. The rest of our team were preparing patches and hauling over the 30 cwt steel plate which will strap the top of the crack when it has, we hope, been closed by floating up the stern. We find much badinage results from having three separate groups sharing two hammers and two saws. The event of the day was a gallant climb up the mainmast by a sergeant of marines, 'Yorky' Tony Stott who took a rope up. Heavy block and tackle were taken up by the crew in the afternoon. Then Horst burnt through the chain taking weight of the yard, and had the tricky job of cutting the swivel without getting crushed when it finally parted. In the process he set the mast on fire with sparks, but the fires were put out without much trouble. It shows how inflammable the old timber is, though. Then the yard was triumphantly lowered in a beautifully judged evolution. It is something to think it has been there since 1872.

Day 3   28 March

Went into Stanley. Unfortunately Horst elected to buy a .22 rifle so the whole expedition was held up for ages whilst he paid numerous visits to the police (both of them) to get a licence. Now no gull, goose, or moving person is safe! Back on board the big sheerlegs was at last erected with all its check wires and eight-part purchase. Meantime the divers had a good day down aft, where all but one of the holes now has a plywood patch outside held on by hook bolts over a piece of angle-iron straddling the hole inside and sealed with a little quick setting cement.

Day 4   Easter Sunday

The pontoon was moved aft in the morning and the lifting of the mizzen mast began. It came up very well after overcoming the initial struggle, but there was more length under water than was expected so it was decided to cut a bit off the bottom where it appeared to be rather rotten anyway. We have taken on a splendid local carpenter, Willie Bowles, who had brought over a chain saw. He found the going very hard. After the first inch the wood was very good. Then he ran into metal and it was opined by some that the mast had a metal core—Strathcona dissenting. By chopping the base away stave by stave it became clear that he had hit one of the numerous horizontal iron pins which hold the mast together.

Eventually he got through on a slightly different line after twice resharpening his saw blade. Meantime a heavy check wire had been put round the base and down onto a block on the lower deck in order to prevent the heel kicking as it came clear of the deck. The carpenter and I had just agreed that the surprisingly good condition of the base at least meant that there was no danger of the mast breaking, when it did just that. It happened quite slowly and the top came straight down on the aft end of the deckhouse which we, particularly me, had been patching up. Luckily I had moved away in case this happened. It was annoying but no harm was done. The remaining masts would, however, be cut at deck level.

Day 5   30 March

By 8 o'clock the wind was about Force eight and very cutting. Too strong for tackling the mainmast. In the evening the mizzen mast was lifted off the deck into the water and towed over to the shore until we are ready to leave. Plans were upset by the failure of the compressor starter motor. We have more or less cleared up the damage at the aft end of the deck house. For the first time I put a foot through the deck today—perhaps a good lesson. No harm done but we have all grown a bit over-confident about walking about other than on the planked walkways. Leslie O'Neil has gone over to Stanley this evening with the compressor starter motor. We hope that the public works department may use similar machines. Darwin arrived yesterday and our people were pleased to get mail. *Sunday Times* sent me envelopes about 24 inches by 15 inches in case they come in useful for posting home 35 mm film.

Day 6   31 March

Much careful locating of the steel pegs in the mast by Horst and then Willie Bowles started cutting with his chain saw. Every so often some pieces were knocked away to free his cut. All went exactly to plan and the mast came down in one piece, when it was set upon to remove the massive iron fittings at the top which are incidentally pretty rotten. It is a beautifully constructed affair, with four main members joined together by pins surrounded by eight smaller staves. With the mast down we covered over the old galley with tin and set up a small stove. This will be the divers and others warming up room, and very much needed at times when the wind is strong and the sun not shining. It will also be used to store gear. Because it has been my particular pigeon, it is known as the Strathcona Arms by some.

Day 7   April 1

The foremast was very reluctant to come down. Willie had to saw three-quarters of the way through or more, and then Horst had to do violent things with the pontoon before it cracked and came down very much under control. But he had great trouble in fitting mast on deck without smashing the old bilge pump mechanism.

Day 8   April 2

The top fitting weighing, I am sure, half a ton was cut off the foremast. To our surprise the mast was pretty sound in spite of not having a lead capping. Not bad after 120 years. It is quite a problem trying to preserve fittings before Horst gets at them with his oxy-acetylene cutter. I have been round with old engine oil and diesel mixed trying to free some of the old shackles, etc. To my surprise I got the winch clutches free without much trouble with the aid of a large hammer. They must have been well greased.

The crack is reported by the divers to extend well beyond the docking keel. This is a lot further than suspected but not altogether unexpected. But, combined with the poor state of the aft bulkheads we are pretty well abandoning the scheme of closing the crack by hinging on the good side. Instead we shall brace very firmly across the crack with massive steel plates (they weigh 1½ tons) and cover the crack as best we can and then pump out all at once. My worry is that if the hull has fallen at the stem, the effect of this strapping will be to make the ship hogged [ends drooping] so that when she is on a level deck there will be a tendency to pull the bottom apart. Fetched sand for our cementing of patches. One of the divers was delighted to find a penguin's egg.

Day 9   3 April

I felt that we suffered from a lack of direction today but I suspect that I often have this feeling through failing to appreciate O'Neil's particular style with his men.

Last night during my daily progress report on the radio I mentioned that we needed old mattresses to pad the patch over the crack. Malcolm managed to condemn some of the marine mattresses and get a special meeting of the public works dept called for 8.30 a.m. to impound some of theirs. A man called Barr gave up two more and Sloggie of the FICo sold us four. All the divers spent the day floundering about as if they were bathing on the Riviera instead of in 40°F. They had a real problem getting the mattresses down because of the buoyancy.

Cement was put into the aft end patch with the result that by this evening there is a pronounced flow of water by the crack. We hope this means there are no other holes. Horst has buoyed a suitable area for submerging the *Mulus*. The divers will inspect the bottom for rocks tomorrow or the next day. Meanwhile all the equipment has been cleared from the deck and docking blocks for the *Great Britain* completed. Progress indeed. April 12 is said to be the anniversary of the day she was beached. We badly want to be back in Stanley by then.

Day 10   4 April

We got the ratchet mechanisms of the windlass free.

Day 11   Low Sunday

A leisurely start as our people were ashore last evening. Three boatloads of sightseers flooded all over the ship getting in the way but not really interfering. Among them Mr Williams, who is the last surviving member of the party that beached her in 1936. A beautiful day—what little I saw of it. Sun quite warm and wind less than usual, dropping all day to a cold and calm evening. The plan is to start pumps tomorrow about midnight, to float about 5 a.m. and probably dock the following night.

Day 13   7 April

Horst last night changed his mind about making an early start this morning so the wind was starting by seven and it rose all morning to a fresh breeze here in Sparrow. About Force 4 to 5 I suppose. Meantime, Horst had decided to lower the *Mulus* from 12 feet freeboard down to about two feet with the result that when finally an attempt was made to move it from alongside the *Great Britain* it proved to be on the bottom. Airlines were therefore rigged from the compressor to start blowing it out again but the tide was still falling so progress was slow and the whole morning was wasted apart from some tidying up.

Day 13 7 April

The ship floated at 5.30 this morning, but there were frustrating preliminaries. I was very keen to get out at least one line to the shore and an anchor before the ship floated but got fobbed off with various excuses until finally at 7 o'clock in the dark two *Varius* crew members and I paddled the Marines' dinghy ashore with great difficulty through the kelp against the wind. We had even more trouble heaving a 3½ inch nylon line ashore with a 4½ inch sisal on the end of it. And then we found we were 200 yards from the holdfast which Horst had set up the day before. Very hard work. The Risdon Beazley men kept pump watch all night aboard the *Great Britain*. The divers carried on plugging leaks all morning until it was quite easy to hold the water level with only the two small spate pumps, but starboard forward and port aft, just below the waterline, were clearly not in very good order as small leaks tended to enlarge rapidly as one tried to plug them. The crack was doing very well. The displacement was closing [it]. The mattresses and ply were excluding all but a very small flow.

Quite suddenly around four the wind started to rise again, from the North-east this time, blowing the ship out of Sparrow Cove. She came afloat unexpectedly and took a sheer to port with both the forward lines bar taut. Horst got very agitated but wouldn't let me ease out the stern line to allow the ship to lie ahead. Luckily the little launch-tug *Lively* had just brought back our generator which had been repaired ashore. She was summoned back by much shouting from Horst into what he calls the 'talky-walky'. At the same moment the *Malvenas* appeared again full of gawpers and was promptly ordered to push on the port bow whilst *Lively* pulled from starboard. This got the situation back under control again, but short of leading out another wire, there did not appear to be any way of consolidating. It was, of course, dark again by now. About six other boats had also come out hoping to see the ship docked. There were some funny moments when the two boats were pulling and pushing madly to starboard whilst I found four Falklanders pulling lustily to port on the rope over to the *Mulus*. We did better once I told them to desist.

Day 14   8 April

It was decided that the *Varius* should go into Stanley for water. We would return to Sparrow Cove that evening. I was delighted because it would re-open the possibility of a docking attempt next morning.

Day 15   9 April

Brunel's birthday. Very little was achieved except for a bit of tidying up.

Day 16   10 April

The pumps had been running all night and the *Great Britain* was afloat but fairly reluctant to come off. Finally her stern shifted and she swung off quite peacefully apart from Horst's inevitable shouting. I fell through the deck for the second time. Much to our consternation nothing would persuade the old ship to go more than 30 feet on to the pontoon, pull and push as the small boats might.

The draft forward must therefore be 11 feet eight inches instead of the predicted 9 feet 9 inches. We had thought we would be OK because the top rudder pintle was showing, and the drawing indicated that this was equivalent to a draft of 12 feet aft which agreed with the 11 feet 9 inches predicted for aft. But there was a tremendous amount of mud in the bottom, as well as old wires, blocks, anchors and chains, two boilers, and a fair size steam engine in pieces. By 8.40 a.m. we had, to my relief, pulled the *Great Britain* back off and tied her up to the aft end of the *Mulus*. The danger was that if the ship got caught on a falling tide she would break her back. We had difficulty persuading Horst that it would be madness to return the *Great Britain* to her old berth and the pumps were more than able to keep her afloat.

The *Mulus* was afloat by noon and submerged again by 2 p.m. with four metres of water over aft at low tide. I had always thought the decision to sink it premature until we had had a chance to check the *Great Britain*'s actual drafts with the divers. Unfortunately the wind came up again in the evening at

45° to the heading of the pontoon and Horst would not try a docking. Meantime Chris Bundes of the *Malvenas* pointed out that the glass had gone lower than he had ever seen in the two years he had owned the ship. This rather confirmed the gale warning on the weather forecast. All we could do was secure the *Great Britain* with adequate lines and hope for the best. Sure enough during the night it reached Force 10 but she rode it beautifully—better than the *Varius* which veered about a good deal.

Day 17   11 April

By morning the wind had dropped and we all felt really confident. It was a comparatively simple job to bring the *Great Britain* up in between the dolphins, but there it became clear that the tide was just not moving at all from the low tide position. The *Varius* was brought up astern and pushed on the port quarter knocking down a couple more guard rail stanchions and pushing over a bollard, whilst the *Malvenas* pushed on the starboard quarter with *Lively* pulling in front. The Marines' launch *Marauder*, and the ship's workboat were tied alongside to help but nothing would move the ship the last 30 feet. However she was now safe and was in a position where the *Mulus* could be blown and re-submerged once more if that really proved necessary as a last resort. But we hoped that the tide would come up enough in the evening and also that the weight of the ship might push the *Mulus* into the mud a little too—but we took other steps in case.

The crew got busy hoisting out some of the masses of old wire and rigging and coiled them up on the double bottom. They ditched some of them before I could get the deadeyes burned off. We also found some compartments in the aft and under the double bottom which appeared to be watertight and these were pumped too. In the event she slid up the last 30 feet with no trouble. The tide had come in and she was six inches lighter so we needn't have waited (as usual) until dark to do the job; but I think Horst must feel it makes it more interesting. In fact she came on six feet further than planned.

Day 18   Sunday 12 April

At 1.30 a.m. .... two loud explosions as inch bolts in the strapping plates sheered. The ship is closing up the crack just as Ewan Corlett predicted. All four pumps started early in the morning to reduce the weight to be lifted by the *Mulus*. By noon the front of the *Mulus* was breaking surface but Leslie O'Neil had got himself marooned in the ship with no ladder long enough to get him down. He is still there as I write—10 p.m. The *Mulus* bow was well out by 2.30 and the ship began to look magnificent as her shape, with which we are all in theory familiar, began to emerge from the water and tower over the stern of the *Varius*. The growth is not as bad as I would have expected. In places whole plates are completely clean. The divers say that the growth and scale come off in one large sheet.

The Colonial Secretary (what a wonderful title) handed over the signed release agreement which he had told me was available having been brought out on *Endurance*. I had wanted to stay aboard until the *Great Britain* was secured. He had kindly not objected to my calling on him on a Sunday morning. His conservatory was over 80°F which they consider cold. There is plenty of sun here in our experience—it's the wind that keeps the temperature down. We also discussed the possibility of our towing the remains of the mizzen mast over to Stanley and trying to get the Marines to erect it with a suitable plaque to commemorate the *Great Britain*'s long stay here. He thought it a good plan but there will be much argument about where to put it. I don't think it will be up when we leave.

Similar discussion continued on when the Governor should visit the *Great Britain* and how we should finally be sent off. It looks as if this may coincide with the Queen's birthday which is a holiday with parades and the full treatment. It is 34 years today that the *Great Britain* was beached. It is a pity we couldn't have got her back to Stanley for the occasion. However, we are still a week ahead of programme at best I think.

Day 19   13 April

The crew were hard at the job of blowing the *Mulus* when I surfaced at 6.20; they had started at 5 o'clock. Horst had sensibly decided against continuing the most delicate part of the surfacing operation, that is bringing up the after part of the pontoon off the ground up to the surface in the dark, but this meant standing about since it is not desirable to have anyone aboard during this process. We all went aboard at 3 p.m. and started driving wedges under the docking keels on the blocks. By teatime at 6 p.m. the ship was well secured and the aft end of the pontoon was breaking surface. Water is seeping surprisingly slowly out of the crack which has closed up to an astonishing extent, pinching in the packing mattresses.

Everyone is vastly impressed with the elegant curved underwater body of the ship—just like a yacht. It now looks vast on the pontoon. Les O'Neil is not enamoured of all the curves because of the problem they will present for his shoring for the trip home. Eventually we decided to stay in Sparrow for the night. Pumping out is not really at the shifting stage yet, and if we go in now we shall have to go alongside the east FICo jetty then move in two days. Furthermore they charge us £50 a day so we shall anchor off until we can go in on the public jetty and stay there.

Day 20   14 April

Horst worked all night on pumping. A miserable night with plenty of wind. The morning was breezy but possible. The pontoon was up enough as both launch and tugs were summoned and arrived at 8.30 a.m. Unfortunately the *Varius* anchor got fouled up with the *Mulus* anchor and we went round and round trying to clear them. By then the wind had increased and there was talk of calling off the move to Stanley. But luckily things improved enough so we moved off with *Varius* alongside to port. *Malvenas* was to starboard and the tugs *Lively* and *Cleo* pulling in front. *Marauder* circled round taking pictures. It was bitterly cold and a South-west wind about force 6. We must have looked quite impressive. Anyway Stanley evidently thought so.

There were 20 or 30 Land Rovers (universal vehicle here) lined up along the shore. Later I heard that they blew their horns and sounded the church bells as we came in, but all we heard was the *John Biscoe*'s ship's whistle. I was hardly ashore when there was a real snow and hail storm with a gale which had been forecast. *Great Britain* and *Mulus* and *Varius* were swinging about through about 180 degrees and everyone thought they must go ashore. Sloggie sent out both the FICo tugs to help, I heard later, but they weren't needed apparently. From ashore I had no way of trying to persuade them to come into the FICo jetty and damn the £50 a day. Met Les O'Neil when he came off in the big launch at 5 o'clock. He reported that all was calm on board and there was no panic.

Day 21   15 April

A quick lunch then aboard at 1.15 p.m. with Leslie O'Neil to find the Captain and Horst at a very low ebb. They were worried at being so near the shore. The anchor was dragging. They had both been on the bridge all night. Another night out there was unthinkable. Horst would prefer to up anchor and go out to the outer harbour of Port William. Finally the whole flotilla got under way about 4.30 p.m. They did a superb job of taking *Mulus* alongside the FICo jetty in a strong wind.

Work went ahead now on making the *Great Britain* secure on the pontoon for the voyage home. Lord Strathcona suggested that they should paint on the white lines and false gunports which was not too enthusiastically received. He went round and collected the few items of Great Britainiana and flew to Darwin, a small Falkland Island settlement, where one of the ship's top-masts is used as a flagstaff and where the FICo uses one of the ship's bells. These were photographed but they were reluctant to part with the bell. Items collected were: an expanding table, a dropleaf table, an oar, a washstand, a commode and bathroom cupboards, a chair, and an ashtray. Madge Biggs, Falklands celebrity, handed over the *Great Britain*'s barometer, and Lord Strathcona got permission to take away what is thought to have been the captain's bath from outside the Government printing office. The Government presented him with a cannon ball.

Visits abroad, and farewell parties over, on:

Day 30   24 April

I was furiously writing the last press release leaning on the mast on the *Mulus* as we eventually took off about 8.45 a.m. As we eased out the *Great Britain*'s rudder came slightly up against the bows of the *Darwin* but there was no weight in it. The wind was rising by now and the pontoon came round very slowly so that we could face down the harbour towards the east. *Cleo* and *Lively,* the two tugs, managed to get themselves into a muddle at one point and both their respective tow ropes had to be cut by quick thinking crew members.

As we skidded through the narrows we were deafened by the hovercraft on one side and a low passing Beaver seaplane over-head. A final glimpse of Stanley and those of us on the *Mulus* climbed on to the *Malvenas,* which put us aboard the *Varius* about ten thirty. The wind was quite fresh and very cold by then. We cleared the lighthouse at about 11 o'clock.'

Leslie O'Neil, aged 56, shipwright and founder member in 1947 of the Royal Navy's post-war Salvage section, looked back and said: 'If you were fanciful and romantic you would say that to watch her floating at the end of the pontoon while we were getting the pontoon turned she would just move into wind and come up between the dolphins and back again, veering just as if she wanted to get on. I don't think we fully appreciated what a fine form of a ship we had because when you see her on the pontoon, particularly when Horst had her with her bow right up, she was like a greyhound.'

There were worrying moments. For Horst the most anxious time was—as always with the pontoon technique—bringing the back end of it up under the ship gently and evenly. Bringing up the front end is easy because the back end on the ground stabilises the unit. But when the back end leaves the ground it has no stability and is more or less out of control. With the contrary winds blowing the *Great Britain* about like a big sail almost anything could have happened. It was during this manoeuvre that the salvage crews saw the proof of Ewan Corlett's theories established. 'There must have been tremendous pressure on that fore part of her whilst Horst was bringing up the stern,' says Leslie O'Neil, 'just like something trying to break her like a stick. If she had been weak, that damaged side would have gone like a carrot. When you look at Horst's pontoon and you look at the indentations along that pontoon plating—that was the weight of the ship.'

For Leslie O'Neil himself: 'The moment when I was most worried was when Horst had her on the pontoon and the pontoon had freeboard and he was still bringing her up and she was careering around in this cove touching the ground almost, and coming away, and the tug drafted as it is couldn't get anywhere near us to help. This was the worrying time when we didn't know whether to go ashore. The weather was forecasting snow and gale winds. We would really have liked more time to get her settled—perhaps a lot of people would think she was not sufficiently supported—but we had to say it's now or never to get her into Port Stanley.'

Lyle Craigie-Halkett, a native Falklander working with Risdon Beazley as a diver, had a third opinion about the trickiest moment: 'They were lucky, because the weather was awful. We had some horrible wind, but it wasn't too persistent. We did get a break now and then. It could have been worse for the time of year. Believe me, Horst and the captain had a real lousy night in

Port Stanley, and I mean lousy. They had to steam ahead on their anchors all night to stop the lot from going on the beach. Against an anchor weighing nearly four tons and nine cables she was veering round as if she was a sail. She would not have stood another day of it. So they had to go all stops out to get her alongside.'

Both Leslie O'Neil and Horst reject the view that more forward planning would have done the job better. 'There is no point in having a plan,' Horst said. 'You have a general line of direction, yes, but there is always something going differently— the weather is not so good, you want three tugs and you have only one, a pump breaks down; with this kind of thing happening it is necessary to deal with situations as they arise.'

For the two team leaders the expedition proved one thing, as Leslie O'Neil said: 'We are the combination that denies the assertion that to be a salvage expert you have to be a master mariner. The only thing about us is that we know how to work hard. Not this business of standing back and saying "do this", and "do that". We work as hard as the lads. Everyone has his own speciality, but you don't find master mariners with strong hands like his—or big ugly ones like these. This pontoon method is an innovation, and the fact that two shipwrights like Horst and me can go down there and do the job is another innovation. As a rule it would have been a master mariner but they have come up the wrong way—they don't learn to work. Talk never does anything in this line of business—it's all hard work and lots of hours. We look ashore and see people paid a lot more than we are—probably the only thing that keeps us going is the interest in the job, and each job being a little bit different. Salvage men certainly don't stay in for the money they get out.'

When the *Varius* and *Mulus* left Stanley for the 7,500-mile 5½-knot journey to Bristol they ran straight into a gale. Leslie O'Neil, who reckons it blew up to 90 knots, said, 'I thought to myself when darkness came the first night, if she was there in the morning she would last to England'. He wanted bad weather to test the security of the ship before the salvage party got off in Montevideo. 'If she had gone for eight days in perfect conditions and we'd left at Montevideo we'd have been a bit conscience-stricken thinking we don't really know how she will stand up. She survived the first night and after that I did not worry too much.'

On 2 May the *Varius* and *Mulus* arrived in Montevideo and the salvage men left. The *Great Britain* set off almost at once for the long last leg. Now she was in the hands almost exclusively of the German crew who had up until then spent most of their time deep sea fishing. Ken Thompson from the Falklands was the only non-German aboard. They saw no ship until after they crossed the Equator; the best speed they achieved was 6½ knots, and an occasional splash of spray went over the *Great Britain*. Three times the *Varius* hauled up close to the pontoon to refuel from the 200 tons of oil stored in one of the tanks. 'Most of the time we spent looking over the stern counting mussels'; this was the *Great Britain*'s last distinction—the best mussels in the Falklands were acknowledged to grow on her rusty plates.

For her first engagement in home waters it had been planned that the *Great Britain* would make a date to sail past Lundy Island at a precise time so that Jack Hayward in an aircraft could see his two redeemed treasures together. Risdon Beazley, proud of its time-keeping on the job so far, hoped that the *Varius* would do her best against persistent head winds to make the appointment. There was hope until the wind changed and blew strongly from the west, blowing the *Great Britain*, sail-like again, so fast that she did, in the end, go past Lundy at night. Just as well, because Jack Hayward would have been displeased with the great white Ulrich Harms painted on the pontoon's sides. He had just sounded off to the *Sunday Express* on his reservations about the German connection. He acknowledges now that without the pontoon the job might have been impossible, and only the Germans had one.

Early on 23 June the *Great Britain* came in sight of Avonmouth. Dried by the winds on her Atlantic voyage, she looked less like a ship than a slab of the Grand Canyon—a precious piece of stratified rock, amber, and sandstone, and jet black streaks. She was escorted by a Royal Navy Reserve minesweeper, and by the Brunel Society in a lifeboat. Eric Gadd, observing a vow not to get his hair cut until the ship came home, somehow got on the *Great Britain*'s deck and jigged about in a top hat. On the way up the Severn the Navy asked an overtaking Italian tanker *Utilitas* to 'Dip your Ensign'. None of the tattered dusters flying from the Italian rigging moved. Its captain must have thought it some kind of British joke, and it was early in the morning for jokes.

A rusty hulk, threadbare and holed precariously propped up on pontoons edging slowly towards Avonmouth in the early sunlight. Long ladders mounted from the pontoon deck up to the *Great Britain*'s sides as if some ancient mariner was actually reconstructing the old ship in a phantom oceanic yard. The Italian's omission was repaired when the *Great Britain* came through the Avonmouth lock into the Royal Edward Dock and all the ships gave Brunel's vessel a solemn welcome on sirens. None blew louder than the *Bristol City*—making up perhaps for the city's 'good riddance' in 1844. There were no great crowds —it was a Tuesday—and only rather awed groups of dockers and office workers saw the pontoon pulled by *Sea Challenge* and *Sea Garth* come into the Avonmouth graving dock. As she went through the locks, some stepped aboard to take away a handful of mussel shells, or a lump of rust.

Work began at once preparing the *Great Britain* for her trip up the Avon on her own bottom. A fussy little steam crane helped with this and brought an appropriate sense of period to the operation. From the bottom of the ship came all sorts of oddments—most valuable of which was what is almost certainly the original anchor. The old engine found in her was laid on the quayside near the colossal masts. The crack in the side—now greatly reduced from the original 14 inches open, ten inches vertical displacement to about half an inch open and one inch vertical displacement—was secured with a sheer web—a solid plate of metal.

There was a bit of bother on 1 July, the day chosen to float the ship off the pontoon. At 4.25 p.m., just as she appeared to float free, the corner of the pontoon left of the ship's port bow suddenly came to the surface, jarring the vessel to starboard and shredding a steel cable securing her to the side of the dock. Ironically the mishap resulted from an attempt to be particularly gentle. Instead of sinking the pontoon it was decided to rest the pontoon on the bottom of the dock and float the ship off it. One of the air-locks had become jammed preventing it from being fully blown. No harm was done.

It was hoped to tow the *Great Britain* up the Avon on Saturday 4 July but the wind touched 20 knots and the trip was cancelled—to the disappointment of thousands who came down by special train and by car. Next morning in a still brisk breeze she set out, tug fore and aft, at seven in the morning to make the seven-mile journey.

The tow was difficult because the *Great Britain* not only had no power of her own, she had no working rudder either. Old as she was she came within three feet of the 325-ft. maximum length for ships in the Avon. All was delicately and successfully achieved, and with much blowing of sirens and dipping of ensigns Brunel's ship passed under Brunel's (posthumous) Clifton suspension bridge. As the ship neared the city the sense of her great size increased. She got through the locks into the floating harbour with not much room to spare—locks largely torn down to let her out in 1844. Copying their forebears' exaggerated fears about getting the *Great Britain* out of harbour, Bristol insisted on £2 million insurance—half against accident in the dry dock, half against blocking the Avon. In vain did the project say that one ship could not succumb to both accidents.

Thousands lined the river bank and the sides of the Avon gorge to see the rejected prodigy return. There were some cheers, much waving—but it was not an ecstatically popular occasion. The vessel had not returned on the penny contribution of ordinary people whose sympathy had been long engaged, whose subscription repeatedly nagged. It was the sudden outcome of determination in high places, made possible by the generosity of an exile millionaire. The city fathers of Bristol came to welcome the ship in the mayoral barge; but in reality Bristol regarded the *Great Britain* as a routine refit for Messrs Charles Hill's yard.

One hundred and twenty-seven years old? Built in Bristol? Designed by Brunel? Maybe, but who is going to provide the car park, the toilets, a £10,000-a-year return on capital invested in two acres of city centre ground needed to service such an attraction? The project points to growing attendances all over Europe —not least 400,000 annually to HMS *Victory*—at museums and historical relics.

The uneasy political background marred none of the ceremonies in Bristol which closed with Prince Philip on board the *Great Britain* as she was tenderly eased back into the Great Western Dock, still miraculously surviving to take back the ship it had been excavated to build. This last short trip took place from Canon's Marsh wharf on the 127th anniversary of the launch by Prince Albert, a day, curiously, when specially high tides made it just possible for the ship again to clear the dock entrance.

Bristol corporation was promoting a   liamentary Bill to close the city docks when the G   in came home— resolving at last the doubts pro   he docks by the antics after her launch. Options   t wide open on development of the area, so t'   while the ship could stay permanently in B'   in the Great Western Dock, and that th   if a move were ordered. No corporation   y would be given or loaned to help restoration.

This last rebuff frosted already cooling relations between the project and city. By summer 1971 national economic difficulties, coupled with the uncertain future of the *Great Britain*, reduced the response to 'old boy net' appeals by the project to industry and commerce. Restoration work slowed down and hopes dwindled of replica masts, funnel, engine room, and saloons appearing soon after a quickly gathered £350,000 had been collected. In July it was announced that permission had been given to moor the *Great Britain* on a pontoon outside the redeveloped St Katharine Dock near Tower Bridge in London.

If Bristol would not adopt the vessel and if she was to be separated from her original dock to go back on a pontoon in Bristol harbour, the project felt that she might as well earn the larger revenues which the capital could generate. There would be risks in moving the ship again; providing and towing the new pontoon would cost more than the original recovery—about £250,000; there was a danger that moored opposite HMS *Belfast* —the Royal Navy's last 'big gun' cruiser—and only a few miles from the *Cutty Sark*, London's appetite for marine archaeology could cloy. Bristol, in spite of everything, remains the first choice of the project for the ship. Falkland Islanders can justify a wry smile as they pass their now empty Sparrow Cove.

Is there a part of the Falklands that is forever *Great Britain*? Lyle Craigie-Halkett doubts it: 'They thought we'd have a go at the ship and lose her or something and mess her up worse than she was. But they've got plenty of wrecks down there. There's dozens. There are about ten or eleven in the harbour alone. The *Britain* did not have any special significance down there. I used to play on it as a kid and I did not know what the hell it was until the job came up really. It was the old *Britain* where you got your arse spanked if you were caught playing on board her.'

Appendix 1

Lloyds Register Report No. 23460 on the *Great Britain* by Will Davey, F. E. Light, and E. C. Wheeler. Liverpool 22 October 1872:

When the iron screw steamship *Great Britain* of Liverpool, 3,270 tons gross measurement, and 1,794 tons register was refitting here in July last, the owners submitted her to our inspection while she was in the graving dock, and at that time the plating was drilled in the several parts as marked in the accompanying sections. They are now desirous of our submitting the results of our examinations to the committee with a view, if possible, to have her classed in our Register Book.

In accordance with their strongly expressed wish we hereby submit the whole of the information relative to this vessel which we can glean, and the results of our survey in this letter, being unable to report her on any of the forms prepared for such purposes, the peculiar construction and absence of any fixed or determinate principle in her design shutting her out from the usual method of submission.

Dimensions as per register: Length, 274 feet; Breadth, 48.2 feet; Depth 31.5 feet. Tonnage under deck, 1,460.48 exclusive of engine room; 2 spaces forward, 60.82; Poop, 273.21; Engine Room, 1,475.48; Horsepower 500.

The girth of the halfmidships section is 48 feet 7½ inches. She was built at Bristol in 1840; poop deck-houses and forecastle were added in 1856, this may almost be termed a spar deck as it is entirely decked over but between poop and forecastle she has thick bulwarks (2 inches) with several ports therein, two for cargo and the others for freeing the wings from water. The so-called spar-deck was doubled in 1869 with 4-inch pine. The main deck was doubled in 1858 with 4-inch pine.

It appears that about 11 years since, or in 1861, the flat of the bottom amidships or under the boiler was mostly renewed, and

in December 1866 the box side stringer on the lower deck, likewise the bulb beams to the main deck; these are truned down
the side and connected to the box stringer by brackets as shown
in the sections.

In July last the fore and aft webs on each side the middle line
for about 50 feet in length in way of the foremast were renewed
as also the iron deck on them. The cement coating in this space
was renewed and the plating and rivetting there seen found in
good order—she had also at that time a new main mast of
pitch pine.

She has no ceiling, consequently the whole of the vessel below
or in the hold could be seen, and the boilers stand high enough
to permit of proper examination. We have seen in the several
sections and have found her in good order; the only place where
oxidation was visible was in the coal bunkers and there only
slight.

The plating is well wrought, and the rivetting good, and
although the butts are single rivetted only they are so close
where seen by us abreast of the forestep that they need no caulking, and have never been caulked. The good rivetting, and the
very peculiar form of the vessel which prevents her carrying an
ordinary quantity of cargo may account for the fact that none of
the butts of the outside plating are visible on her return from
her regular Australian voyages.

Viewing this vessel by the present rules she appears light in
her plating. The main deck beams which are principally of angle
iron (the bulb beams being introduced at various distances) are
extraordinarily trussed diagonally as will be seen from the deck
plan accompanying this report. The webbing in flat of bottom
with the iron deck across and connected to the side well compensate for the usual cross floors.

With all the good qualities which this ship possesses we feel
an indisposition from her age of 30 years in submitting a recommendation to the committee for a classification seeing that the
plating is thin and that an examination has at present been
made of only a part of the vessel, viz., cargo and boiler spaces,
and also feeling that we ought not to judge, at her age, of the
condition of the whole from an inspection of a part, respectfully
submit these remarks and report as requested by the owners for
the committee's consideration suggesting that when the engines
are removed and portions of the passengers' berths a further

survey may be made should the committee, from her construction and thickness of plating (if found not less than now submitted) find her deserving of an A classification subject to a survey annually as well as periodically as required by the rules.

The committee's verdict:

We have carefully examined the two sketches of transverse sections, and a deck plan of this vessel, the particulars given by the Liverpool surveyors, and their very cautious remarks with reference to an A classification. Judging from the information afforded to us and bearing in mind that the parts reported upon are most likely in a better condition than those not seen from the fact of their always being exposed to view, and kept in good condition, we are of opinion that this case is not of that description as to warrant our recommendating any hope being held out by the committee that they would class this vessel A in the register book.

BW
BM   23.10.72

Appendix 2

Original dimensions of the *Great Britain*:

Length overall: 322 ft.
Length of keel: 289 ft.
Beam: 50 ft. 6 in.
Depth of hold 32 ft. 6 in.
Gross tonnage: 3,270.
Laden displacement tonnage, 3,618.
Tonnage, old measurement, 3,444.
Weight of boilers: 200 tons.
Weight of engines: 340 tons.
Weight of wood in the ship: 370 tons.
Carrying capacity: 1,000 tons of coal, 1,000 tons (measurement) of cargo weighing about 400 tons.
Laden draft: 17 ft. forward, 17 ft. 6 in. aft.
Engine room: 116.8 ft. long, 1,919 tons measurement.
1852 Registration: 1,475 tons register; engine room 78.4 ft. long.
1855 Registration—transferred from Bristol to Liverpool: 1,794 tons register.
1882 Registration: 2,735 tons gross, 2,640 tons register.
International Flag Code Letters PJFC.

Appendix 3

Voyage departures:

1. 26 July 1845.
2. 27 September 1845.
3. 9 May 1846.
4. 7 July 1846.
5. 22 September 1846.
These voyages all to New York, USA.
6. 1 May 1852 (New York).
7. 21 August 1852 (Australia).
8. 11 August 1853 (Australia).
9. 28 April 1854 (Australia).
10. March 1855 (Cork, Portsmouth—Malta).
11. 3 September 1855 (Crimea).
12. February 1856 (Liverpool, Cork—Malta).
13. 16 February 1857 (Australia).
14. 8 October 1857 (Cork—Bombay).
15. 28 July 1858 (New York).
16. 21 November 1858 (Australia).
17. 1 July 1859 (New York).
18. Autumn 1859.
19. Spring 1860.
20. 18 July 1860.
21. 17 February 1861.
22. 18 October 1861.
23. 15 June 1862.
24. 19 January 1863.
25. 9 October 1863.
26. 26 April 1864.
27. 19 December 1864.
28. 22 July 1865.
29. 18 February 1866.

30. 25 October 1866.
31. 18 May 1867.
32. 6 July 1868.
33. 1 February 1869.
34. 10 August 1869.
35. 17 March 1870.
36. 30 September 1870.
37. 20 May 1871.
38. 13 December 1871.
39. 24 July 1872.
40. 27 March 1873.
41. 22 October 1873.
42. 1 June 1875.
43. 11 January 1875.
44. 6 August 1875.

The last 27 voyages were all to Australia.

45. November 1882 (San Francisco).
46. 10 June 1884 (San Francisco).
47. 6 February 1886 (Penarth—San Francisco).
48. 24 April 1970 (Falkland Islands—Bristol).

Bibliography

History of Merchant Shipping by W. S. Lindsay. Sampson Low, 1874.

Steam at Sea by K. T. Rowland. David & Charles, 1970.

A Short History of Technology by T. K. Derry and T. I. Williams. Oxford University Press, 1960.

Isambard Kingdom Brunel by L. T. C. Rolt. Longmans, 1957 and Pelican, 1970.

Steamships, the story of their development by R. A. Fletcher. Sidgwick and Jackson, 1910.

A Short History of Naval and Marine Engineering by E. C. Smith. Cambridge University Press, 1938.

The Birth of the Steamboat by H. P. Spratt Griffin, 1958.

A History of Steam Navigation by J. Kennedy. Birchall, 1903.

A History of North Atlantic Steam Navigation by H. Fry. Sampson Low, 1896.

A History of the Port of Bristol by Charles Wells. J. W. Arrowsmith, 1909.

The Life of I. K. Brunel by Isambard Brunel. Longmans, 1870.

The Brunels—Father and Son by Celia Brunel Noble. Cobden Sanderson, 1938.

British Shipping by R. H. Thornton. Cambridge University Press, 1938.

The Origin and Development of Steam Navigation by G. H. Preble. L. R. Hammersley, 1883.

Index